Contents

Foreword ix

Kubla Khan SAMUEL TAYLOR COLERIDGE 3
Byzantium W. B. YEATS 5
'The world is too much with us'
WILLIAM WORDSWORTH 7
Bavarian Gentians D. H. LAWRENCE 8
Bermudas ANDREW MARVELL 9
The Bight ELIZABETH BISHOP 11
Cargoes JOHN MASEFIELD 13
From a Railway Carriage
ROBERT LOUIS STEVENSON 14
'When icicles hang by the wall'
WILLIAM SHAKESPEARE 15
'Sweet Suffolk owl, so trimly dight' ANONYMOUS 16
Adlestrop EDWARD THOMAS 17
'Pleasure it is' WILLIAM CORNISH 18
The Trees PHILIP LARKIN 19
Thistles TED HUGHES 20
Words EDWARD THOMAS 21
The Son GEORGE HERBERT 23
The Earthen Lot TONY HARRISON 24
Quoof PAUL MULDOON 25
Clock a Clay JOHN CLARE 26
Mushrooms SYLVIA PLATH 27
To a Mouse ROBERT BURNS 29
The Mosquito D. H. LAWRENCE 31
Spider HAROLD MASSINGHAM 34

The Tyger WILLIAM BLAKE 35
'For I will consider my Cat Jeoffry'
CHRISTOPHER SMART 36
Poem WILLIAM CARLOS WILLIAMS 40
A Toccata of Galuppi's ROBERT BROWNING 41
Tarantella HILAIRE BELLOC 44
My Papa's Waltz THEODORE ROETHKE 46
Bagpipe Music LOUIS MACNEICE 47
'The splendour falls on castle walls'
ALFRED, LORD TENNYSON 49
Heaven GEORGE HERBERT 50
A Nocturnal Sketch THOMAS HOOD 51
Morning in Madrid BERNARD SPENCER 53
Prelude T. S. ELIOT 54
London Snow ROBERT BRIDGES 55
Hurrahing in Harvest GERARD MANLEY HOPKINS 57
'Flow on, river' WALT WHITMAN 58
Weathers THOMAS HARDY 60
Mariana ALFRED, LORD TENNYSON 61
The Garden of Love WILLIAM BLAKE 64
The Fired Pot ANNA WICKHAM 65
'Still to be neat, still to be dressed' BEN JONSON 66
Love in a Life ROBERT BROWNING 67
La Bella Bona Roba RICHARD LOVELACE 68
Stuffed CAROL ANN DUFFY 69
The Phoenix and the Turtle
WILLIAM SHAKESPEARE 70
The Apparition JOHN DONNE 73
'Her strong enchantments failing' A. E. HOUSMAN 74
Nursery Rhyme of Innocence and Experience
CHARLES CAUSLEY 75
'Proud Maisie is in the wood' SIR WALTER SCOTT 78
The Twa Corbies ANONYMOUS 79

La Belle Dame sans Merci JOHN KEATS 80
The Phantom Horsewoman THOMAS HARDY 82
The Listeners WALTER DE LA MARE 84
Merlin EDWIN MUIR 86
'Batter my heart, three-personed God' JOHN DONNE 87
The Collar GEORGE HERBERT 88
On My First Son BEN JONSON 90
Empty Vessel HUGH MACDIARMID 91
The Emperor of Ice-Cream WALLACE STEVENS 92
Passing the Graveyard ANDREW YOUNG 93
The Childless Father WILLIAM WORDSWORTH 94
The Poplar-Field WILLIAM COWPER 95
Anthem for Doomed Youth WILFRED OWEN 96
'I heard a Fly buzz – when I died' EMILY DICKINSON 97
'Death, be not proud' JOHN DONNE 98
'Do not go gentle into that good night'
DYLAN THOMAS 99
You're SYLVIA PLATH 100
The Birth PAUL MULDOON 101
Full Moon and Little Frieda TED HUGHES 102
Death of a Naturalist SEAMUS HEANEY 103
'A narrow Fellow in the Grass' EMILY DICKINSON 105
Recollections after an Evening Walk JOHN CLARE 106
Dover Beach MATTHEW ARNOLD 108
Lullaby W. H. AUDEN 110
To His Coy Mistress ANDREW MARVELL 112
Dinner with My Mother HUGO WILLIAMS 114
The Thought-Fox TED HUGHES 116
'As kingfishers catch fire'
GERARD MANLEY HOPKINS 117
Anahorish SEAMUS HEANEY 118
Nomad Exquisite WALLACE STEVENS 119
To His Son SIR WALTER RALEGH 120

'Thrice toss these oaken ashes in the air'
THOMAS CAMPION 121
My Cats STEVIE SMITH 122
Our Bias W. H. AUDEN 123
'Like as the waves make towards the pebbled shore'
WILLIAM SHAKESPEARE 124
Remember CHRISTINA ROSSETTI 125
The Sunlight on the Garden LOUIS MACNEICE 126
In the Rhine Valley WENDY COPE 127
'Jenny kiss'd me when we met' LEIGH HUNT 128
'So, we'll go no more a-roving'
GEORGE GORDON, LORD BYRON 129
'Fall, leaves, fall' EMILY BRONTË 130
Sestina ELIZABETH BISHOP 131
'After great pain, a formal feeling comes'
EMILY DICKINSON 133
Exposure WILFRED OWEN 134
Rain EDWARD THOMAS 136
Frost at Midnight SAMUEL TAYLOR COLERIDGE 137
'Now winter nights enlarge' THOMAS CAMPION 140
'In my craft or sullen art' DYLAN THOMAS 141
I Leave This at Your Ear W. S. GRAHAM 142

Notes 143
Acknowledgements 155
Index of Poets 157
Index of First Lines 159

no Jaberwocky ??

Foreword

The main purpose of this book is pleasure. I hope it will be instructive, too, but pleasure is the important thing. If it could have something of the effect on seasoned readers of their first, life-changing encounter with poetry – or, to be more realistic, if it could help reawaken memories of that encounter – then that will do.

Perhaps for some readers it will *be* a first encounter. If so, a word of advice. Mixed in with what I trust will be a large number of immediately appreciable delights, there are bound to be difficulties. Some poetry is obscure, or yields its rewards slowly, but that should not matter if the ear has been sufficiently captivated by the music of the poem in question. There are poets who believe such a slow yielding to be one of the art's defining characteristics. 'Poetry must resist the intelligence almost successfully,' said Wallace Stevens. And T. S. Eliot has explained the process whereby the ear may understand a poem before the mind has been able to grasp it. It is this process with which we are concerned here.

Acres of critical prose, helpful and unhelpful, have been written on the subject of, say, Coleridge's 'Kubla Khan', the first poem in this book. Indeed, it would have been interpreted to death by now, if it wasn't that it was one of the most beautiful-*sounding* poems in the language: a matter not just of its exotic imagery, its invocation of gorgeous names and its impassioned rhetoric, but also of Coleridge's supreme skill in handling its form. By varying line-lengths and shifting the rhyme-scheme, he gives the

poem much of its turbulent momentum and makes it possible for us to go back to it again and again, without feeling that we have got to the bottom of either its musical interest or its meaning.

Because poets are, in this demonstrable respect, technicians, as well as seers, or sufferers, or story-tellers – or whatever else it may be that has led them to express themselves in verse – a certain amount of technical vocabulary is unavoidable when it comes to discussing their work. But not too much. This is no place for pedantry or mystification, and I have tried to keep my notes on the poems (see pages 143–53) brief and jargon-free.

Whenever I have used a term like 'anapaest' or 'quatrain', I have assumed that the reader can get any help he or she may need from an ordinary dictionary. And I have not set out to be either systematic or exhaustive. No doubt a very good anthology, bulkier than this one, could be devoted to showing every conceivable variant of the sonnet form alone, but that would be quite another enterprise. My aim has been to identify poems of outstanding musical quality first, and only to enquire into the metrics if I felt that that might throw light on what the reader was likely already to have picked up for closer examination.

Sometimes, while putting this book together, I have wondered if I haven't been engaged on a rather obvious and superfluous mission: to show that poetry is different from prose. More precisely, I ought to say that it has different *means* and different *ends*. It can do most of the things that prose can do – tell stories, summon up physical descriptions, develop arguments, stir the emotions – but it has another important task as well, and that is to speak to the part of the imagination that is susceptible to the patterning of sounds.

Still obvious? You would hardly think so from the way poetry is liable to be discussed in public. There, it's what can be extracted under the heading of 'content' that gets most of the attention. Yet the poetry lover who was fortunate enough to start in childhood has only to remember his or her first conscious hearing or reading of a poem, and the accompanying surprise that this sort of thing could be – was *allowed* to be – done with words, to feel that the commonly accepted critical procedure cannot really be right.

In all possibility, our hypothetical child discoverer had already noticed that words had a life of their own which went beyond the mere business of exchanging information, stating demands, negotiating daily routines and hazards. Some words were odder than others and had a way of sticking in the mind, long after the occasion for them was past. The fact that certain words sounded alike had also been observed, raising the suspicion that there might be some concealed significance behind such coincidences. Utterances from his or her own mouth had had an effect that was only partly intended, or not intended at all. This strangeness, this palpable otherness, this recalcitrance of words – not unlike the gift of magic when it falls into inexpert hands, in cautionary tales – had already, that is to say, become a matter of some fascination. And here, in that first, momentous encounter with a particular poem, was evidence that someone else had not only observed the same qualities, but done something with them as well.

The poems that get under one's skin in childhood, or at any early stage, should be treated with special respect. I have included a good number here from my own early reading, among them Masefield's 'Cargoes', Shakespeare's 'When icicles hang by the wall', Burns's 'To a Mouse', Edward Thomas's 'Adlestrop' and Keats's 'La Belle Dame

sans Merci'. They are here, not for nostalgic reasons, but because the patterns a young mind could respond to in them turn out to speak with undiminished force to the mature reader capable of analysing their working parts.

For that is how the message comes: in coded form, as *pattern*. Poets are obsessed with pattern. They make patterns, and they break them, with equal deliberateness, and if they are wise, they begin by acquiring a thorough practical knowledge of the patterns other poets have used before them. Knowledge, though, does not necessarily mean imitation; in fact, it seldom does – for what else is the business of 'finding one's own voice' that aspiring poets are constantly being told about, if not implicitly the avoidance of those devices and quirks that have accented, coloured and lent musical individuality to the voices of their antecedents and contemporaries? Taking pains not to be mistaken for another poet does, however, demand appreciation of how that poet came to sound as he or she does, and the common stock of possible means is surprisingly small, when one considers the apparently inexhaustible variety of the results.

Metre, or other, related ways of generating rhythm; the juxtaposition of lines of identical or different lengths; arrangement into stanzas, similarly variable; a handful of inherited forms such as the sonnet, villanelle, sestina and rondeau (all represented here, while the triolet, haiku, pantoum and others are not); rhyme; alliteration and assonance; different kinds of repetition and antithesis – and that's about it, so far as the equipment with which to make your own new noise or music is concerned. Whether you're Shakespeare, or Wordsworth, or Hopkins, or Elizabeth Bishop, or Ted Hughes, that's your tool-kit. So, on with the job and best of luck to you!

These are the terms that recur throughout my notes, which, as the reader will find, frequently amount to little more than jottings, asides, hints as to what to watch out for, signals towards clearer understanding. They are offered in the belief that shop talk, unpretentious discussion of the nuts and bolts of poetic composition, will add to, not take away from, the reader's pleasure in a poem. If you fear that your pleasure may be so spoilt, then leave the notes alone and do your own thinking. I have tried to put the 101 poems that follow in an order that would allow them to keep up a purposeful argument among themselves. If it sounds good to you, that's what matters.

SOUNDS GOOD

SAMUEL TAYLOR COLERIDGE

Kubla Khan

In Xanadu did Kubla Khan
A stately pleasure-dome decree:
Where Alph, the sacred river, ran
Through caverns measureless to man
  Down to a sunless sea.
So twice five miles of fertile ground
With walls and towers were girdled round:
And here were gardens bright with sinuous rills
Where blossomed many an incense-bearing tree;
And here were forests ancient as the hills,
Enfolding sunny spots of greenery.

  But oh! that deep romantic chasm which slanted
Down the green hill athwart a cedarn cover!
A savage place! as holy and enchanted
As e'er beneath a waning moon was haunted
By woman wailing for her demon-lover!
And from this chasm, with ceaseless turmoil seething,
As if this earth in fast thick pants were breathing,
A mighty fountain momently was forced:
Amid whose swift half-intermitted burst
Huge fragments vaulted like rebounding hail,
Or chaffy grain beneath the thresher's flail:
And 'mid these dancing rocks at once and ever
It flung up momently the sacred river.
Five miles meandering with a mazy motion
Through wood and dale the sacred river ran,
Then reached the caverns measureless to man,
And sank in tumult to a lifeless ocean:
And 'mid this tumult Kubla heard from far

Ancestral voices prophesying war!
The shadow of the dome of pleasure
Floated midway on the waves;
Where was heard the mingled measure
From the fountain and the caves.
It was a miracle of rare device,
A sunny pleasure-dome with caves of ice!

A damsel with a dulcimer
In a vision once I saw:
It was an Abyssinian maid,
And on her dulcimer she played,
Singing of Mount Abora.
Could I revive within me
Her symphony and song,
To such a deep delight 'twould win me,
That with music loud and long
I would build that dome in air,
That sunny dome! those caves of ice!
And all who heard should see them there,
And all should cry, Beware! Beware!
His flashing eyes, his floating hair!
Weave a circle round him thrice,
And close your eyes with holy dread,
For he on honey-dew hath fed,
And drunk the milk of Paradise.

Byzantium

· Greek colony, c. 660 BC
· rebuilt by Emperor Constantine, 330 AD

The unpurged images of day recede;
The Emperor's drunken soldiery are abed;
Night resonance recedes, night-walkers' song
After great cathedral gong;
A starlit or a moonlit dome disdains
All that man is,
All mere complexities,
The fury and the mire of human veins.

Before me floats an image, man or shade,
Shade more than man, more image than a shade;
For Hades' bobbin bound in mummy-cloth
May unwind the winding path;
A mouth that has no moisture and no breath
Breathless mouths may summon;
I hail the superhuman;
I call it death-in-life and life-in-death.

Miracle, bird or golden handiwork,
More miracle than bird or handiwork,
Planted on the star-lit golden bough,
Can like the cocks of Hades crow,
Or, by the moon embittered, scorn aloud
In glory of changeless metal
Common bird or petal
And all complexities of mire or blood.

At midnight on the Emperor's pavement flit
Flames that no faggot feeds, nor steel has lit,
Nor storm disturbs, flames begotten of flame,
Where blood-begotten spirits come

And all complexities of fury leave,
Dying into a dance,
An agony of trance,
An agony of flame that cannot singe a sleeve.

Astraddle on the dolphin's mire and blood,
Spirit after spirit! The smithies break the flood,
The golden smithies of the Emperor!
Marbles of the dancing floor
Break bitter furies of complexity,
Those images that yet
Fresh images beget,
That dolphin-torn, that gong-tormented sea.

WILLIAM WORDSWORTH

‘The world is too much with us’

The world is too much with us; late and soon,
Getting and spending, we lay waste our powers:
Little we see in Nature that is ours;
We have given our hearts away, a sordid boon!
This Sea that bares her bosom to the moon;
The winds that will be howling at all hours,
And are up-gathered now like sleeping flowers;
For this, for everything, we are out of tune;
It moves us not. – Great God! I’d rather be
A Pagan suckled in a creed outworn;
So might I, standing on this pleasant lea,
Have glimpses that would make me less forlorn;
Have sight of Proteus rising from the sea;
Or hear old Triton blow his wreathèd horn.

D. H. LAWRENCE

Bavarian Gentians

Not every man has gentians in his house
in soft September, at slow, sad Michaelmas.

Bavarian gentians, big and dark, only dark
darkening the day-time torch-like with the smoking
  blueness of Pluto's gloom,
ribbed and torch-like, with their blaze of darkness spread
  blue
down flattening into points, flattened under the sweep of
  white day,
torch-flower of the blue-smoking darkness, Pluto's dark-
  blue daze,
black lamps from the halls of Dis, burning dark blue,
giving off darkness, blue darkness, as Demeter's pale lamps
  give off light,
lead me then, lead the way.

Reach me a gentian, give me a torch!
let me guide myself with the blue, forked torch of this flower
down the darker and darker stairs, where blue is darkened
  on blueness
even where Persephone goes, just now, from the frosted
  September
to the sightless realm where darkness is awake upon the dark
and Persephone herself is but a voice
or a darkness invisible enfolded in the deeper dark
of the arms Plutonic, and pierced with the passion of
  dense gloom,
among the splendour of torches of darkness, shedding
  darkness on the lost bride and her groom.

ANDREW MARVELL

Bermudas

Where the remote Bermudas ride,
In th' ocean's bosom unespied,
From a small boat, that rowed along,
The listening winds received this song:

'What should we do but sing His praise,
That led us through the watery maze,
Unto an isle so long unknown,
And yet far kinder than our own?
Where He the huge sea-monsters wracks,
That lift the deep upon their backs,
He lands us on a grassy stage,
Safe from the storms, and prelate's rage.
He gave us this eternal spring,
Which here enamels every thing,
And sends the fowls to us in care,
On daily visits through the air.
He hangs in shades the orange bright,
Like golden lamps in a green night,
And does in the pomegranates close
Jewels more rich than Ormus shows.
He makes the figs our mouths to meet,
And throws the melons at our feet;
But apples plants of such a price,
No tree could ever bear them twice.
With cedars chosen by His hand,
From Lebanon, He stores the land,
And makes the hollow seas, that roar,
Proclaim the ambergris on shore.
He cast (of which we rather boast)

The Gospel's pearl upon our coast,
And in these rocks for us did frame
A temple where to sound His name.
Oh! let our voice His praise exalt,
Till it arrive at Heaven's vault,
Which, thence (perhaps) rebounding, may
Echo beyond the Mexique Bay.'

Thus sung they, in the English boat,
An holy and a cheerful note;
And all the way, to guide their chime,
With falling oars they kept the time.

ELIZABETH BISHOP

The Bight

(On my birthday)

At low tide like this how sheer the water is.
White, crumbling ribs of marl protrude and glare
and the boats are dry, the pilings dry as matches.
Absorbing, rather than being absorbed,
the water in the bight doesn't wet anything,
the color of the gas flame turned as low as possible.
One can smell it turning to gas; if one were Baudelaire
one could probably hear it turning to marimba music.
The little ocher dredge at work off the end of the dock
already plays the dry perfectly off-beat claves.
The birds are outsize. Pelicans crash
into this peculiar gas unnecessarily hard,
it seems to me, like pickaxes,
rarely coming up with anything to show for it,
and going off with humorous elbowings.
Black-and-white man-of-war birds soar
on impalpable drafts
and open their tails like scissors on the curves
or tense them like wishbones, till they tremble.
The frowsy sponge boats keep coming in
with the obliging air of retrievers,
bristling with jackstraw gaffs and hooks
and decorated with bobbles of sponges.
There is a fence of chicken wire along the dock
where, glinting like little plowshares,
the blue-gray shark tails are hung up to dry
for the Chinese-restaurant trade.
Some of the little white boats are still piled up

against each other, or lie on their sides, stove in,
and not yet salvaged, if they ever will be, from the last
bad storm,
like torn-open, unanswered letters.
The bight is littered with old correspondences.
Click. Click. Goes the dredge,
and brings up a dripping jawful of marl.
All the untidy activity continues,
awful but cheerful.

JOHN MASEFIELD

Cargoes

Quinquireme of Nineveh from distant Ophir
Rowing home to haven in sunny Palestine,
With a cargo of ivory,
And apes and peacocks,
Sandalwood, cedarwood, and sweet white wine.

Stately Spanish galleon coming from the Isthmus,
Dipping through the Tropics by the palm-green shores,
With a cargo of diamonds,
Emeralds, amethysts,
Topazes, and cinnamon, and gold moidores.

Dirty British coaster with a salt-caked smoke stack
Butting through the Channel in the mad March days,
With a cargo of Tyne coal,
Road-rail, pig-lead,
Firewood, iron-ware, and cheap tin trays.

ROBERT LOUIS STEVENSON

From a Railway Carriage

Faster than fairies, faster than witches,
Bridges and houses, hedges and ditches;
And charging along like troops in a battle,
All through the meadows the horses and cattle:
All of the sights of the hill and the plain
Fly as thick as driving rain;
And ever again, in the wink of an eye,
Painted stations whistle by.

Here is a child who clambers and scrambles,
All by himself and gathering brambles;
Here is a tramp who stands and gazes;
And there is the green for stringing the daisies!
Here is a cart run away in the road
Lumping along with man and load;
And here is a mill and there is a river.
Each a glimpse and gone for ever!

'When icicles hang by the wall'

When icicles hang by the wall,
  And Dick the shepherd blows his nail,
And Tom bears logs into the hall,
  And milk comes frozen home in pail,
When blood is nipped, and ways be foul,
Then nightly sings the staring owl,
    Tu-whit, tu-who!
    A merry note,
While greasy Joan doth keel the pot.

When all around the wind doth blow,
  And coughing drowns the parson's saw,
And birds sit brooding in the snow,
  And Marian's nose looks red and raw,
When roasted crabs hiss in the bowl,
Then nightly sings the staring owl,
    Tu-whit, to-who!
    A merry note,
While greasy Joan doth keel the pot.

ANONYMOUS

'Sweet Suffolk owl, so trimly dight'

Sweet Suffolk owl, so trimly dight
With feathers, like a lady bright,
Thou sing'st alone, sitting by night,
Te whit, te whoo! Te whit, te whoo!

Thy note, that forth so freely rolls,
With shrill command the mouse controls;
And sings a dirge for dying souls,
Te whit, te whoo! Te whit, te whoo!

dight: adorned

EDWARD THOMAS

Adlestrop

Yes. I remember Adlestrop –
The name, because one afternoon
Of heat the express-train drew up there
Unwontedly. It was late June.

The steam hissed. Someone cleared his throat.
No one left and no one came
On the bare platform. What I saw
Was Adlestrop – only the name

And willows, willow-herb, and grass,
And meadowsweet, and haycocks dry,
No whit less still and lonely fair
Than the high cloudlets in the sky.

And for that minute a blackbird sang
Close by, and round him, mistier,
Farther and farther, all the birds
Of Oxfordshire and Gloucestershire.

WILLIAM CORNISH

'Pleasure it is'

Pleasure it is
        To hear, iwis,
    The birdes sing.
The deer in the dale,
The sheep in the vale,
    The corn springing;
God's purveyance
For sustenance
    It is for man.
Then we always
To Him give praise,
    And thank Him than,
    And thank Him than.

iwis: truly, certainly; *than*: then

The Trees

The trees are coming into leaf
Like something almost being said;
The recent buds relax and spread,
Their greenness is a kind of grief.

Is it that they are born again
And we grow old? No, they die too.
Their yearly trick of looking new
Is written down in rings of grain.

Yet still the unresting castles thresh
In fullgrown thickness every May.
Last year is dead, they seem to say,
Begin afresh, afresh, afresh.

Thistles

Against the rubber tongues of cows and the hoeing hands of men
Thistles spike the summer air
Or crackle open under a blue-black pressure.

Every one a revengeful burst
Of resurrection, a grasped fistful
Of splintered weapons and Icelandic frost thrust up

From the underground stain of a decayed Viking.
They are like pale hair and the gutturals of dialects.
Every one manages a plume of blood.

Then they grow grey, like men.
Mown down, it is a feud. Their sons appear,
Stiff with weapons, fighting back over the same ground.

EDWARD THOMAS

Words

Out of us all
That make rhymes,
Will you choose
Sometimes –
As the winds use
A crack in a wall
Or a drain,
Their joy or their pain
To whistle through –
Choose me,
You English words?

I know you:
You are light as dreams,
Tough as oak,
Precious as gold,
As poppies and corn,
Or an old cloak:
Sweet as our birds
To the ear,
As the burnet rose
In the heat
Of Midsummer:
Strange as the races
Of dead and unborn:
Strange and sweet
Equally,
And familiar,
To the eye,
As the dearest faces

That a man knows,
And as lost homes are:
But though older far
Than oldest yew, –
As our hills are, old, –
Worn new
Again and again:
Young as our streams
After rain:
And as dear
As the earth which you prove
That we love.

Make me content
With some sweetness
From Wales
Whose nightingales
Have no wings, –
From Wiltshire and Kent
And Herefordshire,
And the villages there, –
From the names, and the things
No less.
Let me sometimes dance
With you,
Or climb
Or stand perchance
In ecstasy,
Fixed and free
In a rhyme,
As poets do.

GEORGE HERBERT

The Son

Let foreign nations of their language boast,
What fine variety each tongue affords:
I like our language, as our men and coast;
Who cannot dress it well, want wit, not words.
How neatly do we give one only name
To parent's issue and the sun's bright star!
A son is light and fruit; a fruitful flame
Chasing the Father's dimness, carried far
From the first man in th' East, to fresh and new
Western discov'ries of posterity.
So in one word our Lord's humility
We turn upon him in a sense most true:
  For what Christ once in humbleness began,
  We him in glory call, *The Son of Man*.

TONY HARRISON

The Earthen Lot

for Alistair Elliot

'From Isphahan to Northumberland, there is no building that does not show the influence of that oppressed and neglected herd of men.'

William Morris, *The Art of the People*

Sand, caravans, and teetering sea-edge graves.

The seaward side's for those of lowly status.
Not only gales gnaw at their names, the waves
Jostle the skulls and bones from their quietus.

The Church is a solid bulwark for their betters
against the scouring sea-salt that erodes
these chiselled sandstone formal Roman letters
to flowing calligraphic Persian odes,
singing of sherbet, sex in Samarkand,
with Hafiz at the hammams and harems,
O anywhere but bleak Northumberland
with responsibilities for others' dreams!

Not for the Northern bard the tamarinds
where wine is always cool, and *kusi* hot –

his line from Omar scrivened by this wind 's:

Some could articulate, while others not.

(Newbiggin-by-the-Sea, 1977)

Quoof

How often have I carried our family word
for the hot water bottle
to a strange bed,
as my father would juggle a red-hot half-brick
in an old sock
to his childhood settle.
I have taken it into so many lovely heads
or laid it between us like a sword.

An hotel room in New York City
with a girl who spoke hardly any English,
my hand on her breast
like the smouldering one-off spoor of the yeti
or some other shy beast
that has yet to enter the language.

JOHN CLARE

Clock a Clay

In the cowslips peeps I lye
Hidden from the buzzing fly
While green grass beneath me lies
Pearled wi' dew like fishes eyes
Here I lye a Clock a clay
Waiting for the time o' day

While grassy forests quake surprise
And the wild wind sobs and sighs
My gold home rocks as like to fall
On its pillars green and tall
When the pattering rain drives bye
Clock a Clay keeps warm and dry

Day by day and night by night
All the week I hide from sight
In the cowslips peeps I lye
In rain and dew still warm and dry
Day and night and night and day
Red black spotted clock a clay

My home it shakes in wind and showers
Pale green pillar top't wi' flowers
Bending at the wild winds breath
Till I touch the grass beneath
Here still I live lone clock a clay
Watching for the time of day

Clock a Clay: ladybird

Mushrooms

Overnight, very
Whitely, discreetly,
Very quietly

Our toes, our noses
Take hold on the loam,
Acquire the air.

Nobody sees us,
Stops us, betrays us;
The small grains make room.

Soft fists insist on
Heaving the needles,
The leafy bedding,

Even the paving.
Our hammers, our rams,
Earless and eyeless,

Perfectly voiceless,
Widen the crannies,
Shoulder through holes. We

Diet on water,
On crumbs of shadow,
Bland-mannered, asking

Little or nothing.
So many of us!
So many of us!

We are shelves, we are
Tables, we are meek,
We are edible,

Nudgers and shovers
In spite of ourselves.
Our kind multiplies:

We shall by morning
Inherit the earth.
Our foot's in the door.

To a Mouse

On Turning Her Up in Her Nest, with the Plough, November 1785

Wee, sleekit, cowrin, tim'rous beastie,
O, what a panic's in thy breastie!
Thou need na start awa sae hasty,
    Wi' bickering brattle!
I wad be laith to rin an' chase thee,
    Wi' murd'ring pattle!

I'm truly sorry Man's dominion
Has broken Nature's social union,
An' justifies that ill opinion,
    Which makes thee startle,
At me, thy poor, earth-born companion,
    An' fellow-mortal!

I doubt na, whyles, but thou may thieve;
What then? poor beastie, thou maun live!
A daimen icker in a thrave
    'S a sma' request.
I'll get a blessin wi' the lave,
    An' never miss't!

Thy wee-bit housie, too, in ruin!
Its silly wa's the win's are strewin!
An' naething, now, to big a new ane,
    O' foggage green!
An' bleak December's winds ensuin,
    Baith snell an' keen!

Thou saw the fields laid bare an' waste,
An' weary Winter comin fast,
An' cozie here, beneath the blast,
Thou thought to dwell,
Till crash! the cruel coulter past
Out thro' thy cell.

That wee-bit heap o' leave an' stibble
Has cost thee monie a weary nibble!
Now thou's turn'd out, for a' thy trouble,
But house or hald,
To thole the Winter's sleety dribble,
An' cranreuch cauld!

But, Mousie, thou art no thy lane,
In proving foresight may be vain:
The best-laid schemes o' Mice an' Men
Gang aft a-gley,
An' lea'e us nought but grief an' pain,
For promis'd joy!

Still thou art blest, compar'd wi' me!
The present only toucheth thee:
But, Och! I backward cast my e'e
On prospects drear!
An' forward, tho' I canna see,
I guess an' fear!

brattle: scamper; *pattle*: kind of spade; *whyles*: sometimes; *daimen icker*: occasional ear of corn; *thrave*: two stooks' worth; *lave*: remainder; *big*: build; *foggage*: rank grass; *snell*: bitter; *coulter*: blade in front of ploughshare; *But*: without; *hald*: refuge; *thole*: endure; *cranreuch*: hoar-frost; *thy lane*: on your own; *gang aft a-gley*: often go awry

The Mosquito

When did you start your tricks,
Monsieur?

What do you stand on such high legs for?
Why this length of shredded shank,
You exaltation?

Is it so that you shall lift your centre of gravity upwards
And weigh no more than air as you alight upon me,
Stand upon me weightless, you phantom?

I heard a woman call you the Winged Victory
In sluggish Venice.
You turn your head towards your tail, and smile.

How can you put so much devilry
Into that translucent phantom shred
Of a frail corpus?

Queer, with your thin wings and your streaming legs,
How you sail like a heron, or a dull clot of air,
A nothingness.

Yet what an aura surrounds you;
Your evil little aura, prowling, and casting a numbness on
my mind.

That is your trick, your bit of filthy magic:
Invisibility, and the anaesthetic power
To deaden my attention in your direction.

But I know your game now, streaky sorcerer.
Queer, how you stalk and prowl the air
In circles and evasions, enveloping me,
Ghoul on wings
Winged Victory.

Settle, and stand on long thin shanks
Eyeing me sideways, and cunningly conscious that I am
aware,
You speck.

I hate the way you lurch off sideways into air
Having read my thoughts against you.

Come then, let us play at unawares,
And see who wins in this sly game of bluff.
Man or mosquito.

You don't know that I exist, and I don't know that you
exist.
Now then!

It is your trump,
It is your hateful little trump,
You pointed fiend,
Which shakes my sudden blood to hatred of you:
It is your small, high, hateful bugle in my ear.

Why do you do it?
Surely it is bad policy.

They say you can't help it.

If that is so, then I believe a little in Providence protecting
the innocent.
But it sounds so amazingly like a slogan,
A yell of triumph as you snatch my scalp.

Blood, red blood
Super-magical
Forbidden liquor.

I behold you stand
For a second enspasmed in oblivion,
Obscenely ecstasied
Sucking live blood,
My blood.

Such silence, such suspended transport,
Such gorging,
Such obscenity of trespass.

You stagger
As well as you may.
Only your accursed hairy frailty,
Your own imponderable weightlessness
Saves you, wafts you away on the very draught my anger
makes in its snatching.

Away with a paean of derision,
You winged blood-drop.

Can I not overtake you?
Are you one too many for me,
Winged Victory?
Am I not mosquito enough to out-mosquito you?

Queer, what a big stain my sucked blood makes
Beside the infinitesimal faint smear of you!
Queer, what a dim dark smudge you have disappeared
into!

HAROLD MASSINGHAM

Spider

Trickling rope-trickster,
You could almost vanish
In this mirage-weather.

You know the knack, don't you?
Imagination's envy.
You're your own yoyo, aren't you?

Born to no distraction –
You better most of us
In pretty design,

Are versatile:
Have made frosty doilies,
Could rig a galleon-model;

And also, with more ingenuity,
Have made a circus safety-net
For the hurtling fly.

WILLIAM BLAKE

The Tyger

Tyger! Tyger! burning bright
In the forests of the night,
What immortal hand or eye
Could frame thy fearful symmetry?

In what distant deeps or skies
Burnt the fire of thine eyes?
On what wings dare he aspire?
What the hand dare sieze the fire?

And what shoulder, & what art,
Could twist the sinews of thy heart?
And when thy heart began to beat,
What dread hand? & what dread feet?

What the hammer? what the chain?
In what furnace was thy brain?
What the anvil? what dread grasp
Dare its deadly terrors clasp?

When the stars threw down their spears,
And water'd heaven with their tears,
Did he smile his work to see?
Did he who made the Lamb make thee?

Tyger! Tyger! burning bright
In the forests of the night,
What immortal hand or eye
Dare frame thy fearful symmetry?

'For I will consider my Cat Jeoffry'

(*from* Jubilate Agno)

For I will consider my Cat Jeoffry.
For he is the servant of the Living God duly and daily
serving him.
For at the first glance of the glory of God in the East he
worships in his way.
For is this done by wreathing his body seven times round
with elegant quickness.
For then he leaps up to catch the musk, which is the
blessing of God upon his prayer.
For he rolls upon prank to work it in.
For having done duty and received blessing he begins to
consider himself.
For this he performs in ten degrees.
For first he looks upon his fore-paws to see if they are clean.
For secondly he kicks up behind to clear away there.
For thirdly he works it upon stretch with the fore paws
extended.
For fourthly he sharpens his paws by wood.
For fifthly he washes himself.
For Sixthly he rolls upon wash.
For Seventhly he fleas himself, that he may not be
interrupted upon the beat.
For Eighthly he rubs himself against a post.
For Ninthly he looks up for his instructions.
For Tenthly he goes in quest of food.
For having consider'd God and himself he will consider his
neighbour.
For if he meets another cat he will kiss her in kindness.

For when he takes his prey he plays with it to give it
chance.
For one mouse in seven escapes by his dallying.
For when his day's work is done his business more properly
begins.
For he keeps the Lord's watch in the night against the
adversary.
For he counteracts the powers of darkness by his electrical
skin and glaring eyes.
For he counteracts the Devil, who is death, by brisking
about the life.
For in his morning orisons he loves the sun and the sun
loves him.
For he is of the tribe of Tiger.
For the Cherub Cat is a term of the Angel Tiger.
For he has the subtlety and hissing of a serpent, which in
goodness he suppresses.
For he will not do destruction, if he is well-fed, neither will
he spit without provocation.
For he purrs in thankfulness, when God tells him he's a
good Cat.
For he is an instrument for the children to learn
benevolence upon.
For every house is incompleat without him and a blessing
is lacking in the spirit.
For the Lord commanded Moses concerning the cats at the
departure of the Children of Israel from Egypt.
For every family had one cat at least in the bag.
For the English Cats are the best in Europe.
For he is the cleanest in the use of his fore-paws of any
quadrupede.
For the dexterity of his defence is an instance of the love of
God to him exceedingly.

For he is the quickest to his mark of any creature.
For he is tenacious of his point.
For he is a mixture of gravity and waggery.
For he knows that God is his Saviour.
For there is nothing sweeter than his peace when at rest.
For there is nothing brisker than his life when in motion.
For he is of the Lord's poor and so indeed is he called by benevolence perpetually – Poor Jeoffry! poor Jeoffry! the rat has bit thy throat.
For I bless the name of the Lord Jesus that Jeoffry is better.
For the divine spirit comes about his body to sustain it in compleat cat.
For his tongue is exceeding pure so that it has in purity what it wants in musick.
For he is docile and can learn certain things.
For he can set up with gravity which is patience upon approbation.
For he can fetch and carry, which is patience in employment.
For he can jump over a stick which is patience upon proof positive.
For he can spraggle upon waggle at the word of command.
For he can jump from an eminence into his master's bosom.
For he can catch the cork and toss it again.
For he is hated by the hypocrite and miser.
For the former is afraid of detection.
For the latter refuses the charge.
For he camels his back to bear the first notion of business.
For he is good to think on, if a man would express himself neatly.
For he made a great figure in Egypt for his signal services.
For he killed the Ichneumon-rat very pernicious by land.

For his ears are so acute that they sting again.
For from this proceeds the passing quickness of his attention.
For by stroaking of him I have found out electricity.
For I perceived God's light about him both wax and fire.
For the Electrical fire is the spiritual substance, which God sends from heaven to sustain the bodies both of man and beast.
For God has blessed him in the variety of his movements.
For, tho he cannot fly, he is an excellent clamberer.
For his motions upon the face of the earth are more than any other quadrupede.
For he can tread to all the measures upon the musick.
For he can swim for life.
For he can creep.

Poem

As the cat
climbed over
the top of

the jamcloset
first the right
forefoot

carefully
then the hind
stepped down

into the pit of
the empty
flowerpot

A Toccata of Galuppi's

Oh Galuppi, Baldassaro, this is very sad to find!
I can hardly misconceive you; it would prove me deaf and
blind;
But although I take your meaning, 't is with such a heavy
mind!

Here you come with your old music, and here's all the good
it brings.
What, they lived once thus at Venice where the merchants
were the kings,
Where Saint Mark's is, where the Doges used to wed
the sea with rings?

Ay, because the sea's the street there; and 't is arched by ...
what you call
... Shylock's bridge with houses on it, where they kept the
carnival:
I was never out of England – it's as if I saw it all.

Did young people take their pleasure when the sea was
warm in May?
Balls and masks begun at midnight, burning ever to
mid-day,
When they made up fresh adventures for the morrow, do
you say?

Was a lady such a lady, cheeks so round and lips so red, –
On her neck the small face buoyant, like a bell-flower on its
bed,
O'er the breast's superb abundance where a man might
base his head?

Well, and it was graceful of them – they'd break talk off and
afford
– She, to bite her mask's black velvet – he, to finger on his
sword,
While you sat and played Toccatas, stately at the
clavichord?

What? Those lesser thirds so plaintive, sixths diminished,
sigh on sigh,
Told them something? Those suspensions, those solutions
– 'Must we die?'
Those commiserating sevenths – 'Life might last! we can
but try!'

'Were you happy?' – 'Yes.' – 'And are you still as happy?' –
'Yes. And you?'
– 'Then, more kisses!' – 'Did *I* stop them, when a million
seemed so few?'
Hark, the dominant's persistence till it must be answered
to!

So, an octave struck the answer. Oh, they praised you,
I dare say!
'Brave Galuppi! that was music! good alike at grave and
gay!
I can always leave off talking when I hear a master play!'

Then they left you for their pleasure: till in due time, one
by one,
Some with lives that came to nothing, some with deeds as
well undone,
Death stepped tacitly and took them where they never see
the sun.

But when I sit down to reason, think to take my stand nor
swerve,
While I triumph o'er a secret wrung from nature's close
reserve,
In you come with your cold music till I creep thro' every
nerve.

Yes, you, like a ghostly cricket, creaking where a house
was burned:
'Dust and ashes, dead and done with, Venice spent what
Venice earned.
The soul, doubtless, is immortal – where a soul can be
discerned.'

'Yours for instance: you know physics, something of
geology,
Mathematics are your pastime; souls shall rise in their
degree;
Butterflies may dread extinction, – you'll not die, it cannot
be!'

'As for Venice and her people, merely born to bloom and
drop,
Here on earth they bore their fruitage, mirth and folly were
the crop:
What of soul was left, I wonder, when the kissing had to
stop?'

'Dust and ashes!' So you creak it, and I want the heart to
scold.
Dear dead women, with such hair, too – what's become of
all the gold
Used to hang and brush their bosoms? I feel chilly and
grown old.

Tarantella

Do you remember an Inn,
Miranda?
Do you remember an Inn?
And the tedding and the spreading
Of the straw for a bedding,
And the fleas that tease in the High Pyrenees,
And the wine that tasted of the tar?
And the cheers and the jeers of the young muleteers
(Under the dark of the vine verandah)?
Do you remember an Inn, Miranda,
Do you remember an Inn?
And the cheers and the jeers of the young muleteers
Who hadn't got a penny,
And who weren't paying any,
And the hammer at the doors and the Din?
And the Hip! Hop! Hap!
Of the clap
Of the hands to the twirl and the swirl
Of the girl gone chancing,
Glancing,
Dancing,
Backing and advancing,
Snapping of the clapper to the spin
Out and in –
And the Ting, Tong, Tang of the guitar!
Do you remember an Inn,
Miranda?
Do you remember an Inn?

Never more;
Miranda,
Never more.
Only the high peaks hoar:
And Aragon a torrent at the door.
No sound
In the walls of the Halls where falls
The tread
Of the feet of the dead to the ground.
No sound:
Only the boom
Of the far Waterfall like Doom.

THEODORE ROETHKE

My Papa's Waltz

The whiskey on your breath
Could make a small boy dizzy;
But I hung on like death:
Such waltzing was not easy.

We romped until the pans
Slid from the kitchen shelf;
My mother's countenance
Could not unfrown itself.

The hand that held my wrist
Was battered on one knuckle;
At every step you missed
My right ear scraped a buckle.

You beat time on my head
With a palm caked hard by dirt,
Then waltzed me off to bed
Still clinging to your shirt.

LOUIS MACNEICE

Bagpipe Music

It's no go the merrygoround, it's no go the rickshaw,
All we want is a limousine and a ticket for the peepshow.
Their knickers are made of crêpe-de-chine, their shoes are made of python,
Their halls are lined with tiger rugs and their walls with heads of bison.

John MacDonald found a corpse, put it under the sofa,
Waited till it came to life and hit it with a poker,
Sold its eyes for souvenirs, sold its blood for whiskey,
Kept its bones for dumb-bells to use when he was fifty.

It's no go the Yogi-Man, it's no go Blavatsky,
All we want is a bank balance and a bit of skirt in a taxi.

Annie MacDougall went to milk, caught her foot in the heather,
Woke to hear a dance record playing of Old Vienna.
It's no go your maidenheads, it's no go your culture,
All we want is a Dunlop tyre and the devil mend the puncture.

The Laird o' Phelps spent Hogmanay declaring he was sober,
Counted his feet to prove the fact and found he had one foot over.
Mrs Carmichael had her fifth, looked at the job with repulsion,
Said to the midwife 'Take it away; I'm through with over-production'.

It's no go the gossip column, it's no go the Ceilidh,
All we want is a mother's help and a sugar-stick for the baby.

Willie Murray cut his thumb, couldn't count the damage,
Took the hide of an Ayrshire cow and used it for a bandage.
His brother caught three hundred cran when the seas were lavish,
Threw the bleeders back in the sea and went upon the parish.

It's no go the Herring Board, it's no go the Bible,
All we want is a packet of fags when our hands are idle.

It's no go the picture palace, it's no go the stadium,
It's no go the country cot with a pot of pink geraniums,
It's no go the Government grants, it's no go the elections,
Sit on your arse for fifty years and hang your hat on a pension.

It's no go my honey love, it's no go my poppet;
Work your hands from day to day, the winds will blow the profit.
The glass is falling hour by hour, the glass will fall for ever,
But if you break the bloody glass you won't hold up the weather.

'The splendour falls on castle walls'

(*from* The Princess)

The splendour falls on castle walls
  And snowy summits old in story:
The long light shakes across the lakes,
  And the wild cataract leaps in glory.
Blow, bugle, blow, set the wild echoes flying,
Blow, bugle; answer, echoes, dying, dying, dying.

O hark, O hear! how thin and clear,
  And thinner, clearer, farther going!
O sweet and far from cliff and scar
  The horns of Elfland faintly blowing!
Blow, let us hear the purple glens replying:
Blow, bugle; answer, echoes, dying, dying, dying.

O love, they die in yon rich sky,
  They faint on hill or field or river:
Our echoes roll from soul to soul,
  And grow for ever and for ever.
Blow, bugle, blow, set the wild echoes flying,
And answer, echoes, answer, dying, dying, dying.

Heaven

O who will show me those delights on high?
    ECHO.   *I.*
Thou Echo, thou art mortal, all men know.
    ECHO.   *No.*
Wert thou not born among the trees and leaves?
    ECHO.   *Leaves.*
And are there any leaves, that still abide?
    ECHO.   *Bide.*
What leaves are they? impart the matter wholly.
    ECHO.   *Holy.*
Are holy leaves the Echo then of bliss?
    ECHO.   *Yes.*
Then tell me, what is that supreme delight?
    ECHO.   *Light.*
Light to the mind: what shall the will enjoy?
    ECHO.   *Joy.*
But are there cares and business with the pleasure?
    ECHO.   *Leisure.*
Light, joy, and leisure; but shall they persever?
    ECHO.   *Ever.*

THOMAS HOOD

A Nocturnal Sketch

Even is come; and from the dark Park, hark,
The signal of the setting sun – one gun!
And six is sounding from the chime, prime time
To go and see the Drury-Lane Dane slain, –
Or hear Othello's jealous doubt spout out, –
Or Macbeth raving at that shade-made blade,
Denying to his frantic clutch much touch; –
Or else to see Ducrow with wide stride ride
Four horses as no other man can span;
Or in the small Olympic Pit, sit split
Laughing at Liston, while you quiz his phiz.
Anon Night comes, and with her wings brings things
Such as, with his poetic tongue, Young sung;
The gas up-blazes with its bright white light,
And paralytic watchmen prowl, howl, growl,
About the streets and take up Pall-Mall Sal,
Who, hasting to her nightly jobs, robs fobs.

Now thieves to enter for your cash, smash, crash,
Past drowsy Charley in a deep sleep, creep,
But frightened by Policeman B 3, flee,
And while they're going, whisper low, 'No go!'
Now puss, while folks are in their beds, treads leads.
And sleepers waking, grumble – 'Drat that cat!'
Who in the gutter caterwauls, squalls, mauls
Some feline foe, and screams in shrill ill-will.

Now Bulls of Bashan, of a prize size, rise
In childish dreams, and with a roar gore poor
Georgy, or Charley, or Billy, willy-nilly; –

But Nursemaid, in a nightmare rest, chest-pressed,
Dreameth of one of her old flames, James Games,
And that she hears – what faith is man's! – Ann's banns
And his, from Reverend Mr Rice, twice, thrice:
White ribbons flourish, and a stout shout out,
That upward goes, shows Rose knows those bows' woes!

BERNARD SPENCER

Morning in Madrid

Skirmish of wheels and bells and someone calling.
A donkey's bronchial greeting, groan and whistle,
the weeping factory sirens rising, falling.

Yelping of engines from the railyard drifted:
then, prelude to the gold-of-wine of morning,
the thunderstorm of iron shutters lifted.

Prelude

The winter evening settles down
With smell of steaks in passageways.
Six o'clock.
The burnt-out ends of smoky days.
And now a gusty shower wraps
The grimy scraps
Of withered leaves about your feet
And newspapers from vacant lots;
The showers beat
On broken blinds and chimney-pots,
And at the corner of the street
A lonely cab-horse steams and stamps.

And then the lighting of the lamps.

London Snow

When men were all asleep the snow came flying,
In large white flakes falling on the city brown,
Stealthily and perpetually settling and loosely lying,
  Hushing the latest traffic of the drowsy town;
Deadening, muffling, stifling its murmurs failing;
Lazily and incessantly floating down and down:
  Silently sifting and veiling road, roof and railing;
Hiding difference, making unevenness even,
Into angles and crevices softly drifting and sailing.
  All night it fell, and when full inches seven
It lay in the depth of its uncompacted lightness,
The clouds blew off from a high and frosty heaven;
  And all woke earlier for the unaccustomed brightness
Of the winter dawning, the strange unheavenly glare:
The eye marvelled – marvelled at the dazzling whiteness;
  The ear hearkened to the stillness of the solemn air;
No sound of wheel rumbling nor of foot falling,
And the busy morning cries came thin and spare.
  Then boys I heard, as they went to school, calling,
They gathered up the crystal manna to freeze
Their tongues with tasting, their hands with snowballing;
  Or rioted in a drift, plunging up to the knees;
Or peering up from under the white-mossed wonder,
'O look at the trees!' they cried, 'O look at the trees!'
  With lessened load a few carts creak and blunder,
Following along the white deserted way,
A country company long dispersed asunder:
  When now already the sun, in pale display
Standing by Paul's high dome, spread forth below

His sparkling beams, and awoke the stir of the day.
For now doors open, and war is waged with the snow;
And trains of sombre men, past tale of number,
Tread long brown paths, as toward their toil they go:
But even for them awhile no cares encumber
Their minds diverted; the daily word is unspoken,
The daily thoughts of labour and sorrow slumber
At the sight of the beauty that greets them, for the charm
they have broken.

Hurrahing in Harvest

Summer ends now; now, barbarous in beauty, the stooks
  rise
Around; up above, what wind-walks! what lovely
  behaviour
Of silk-sack clouds! has wilder, wilful-wavier
Meal-drift moulded ever and melted across skies?

I walk, I lift up, I lift up heart, eyes,
Down all that glory in the heavens to glean our Saviour;
And, éyes, heárt, what looks, what lips yet gave you a
Rapturous love's greeting of realer, of rounder replies?

And the azurous hung hills are his world-wielding
  shoulder
Majestic – as a stallion stalwart, very-violet-sweet! –
These things, these things were here and but the beholder
Wanting; which two when they once meet,
The heart rears wings bold and bolder
And hurls for him, O half hurls earth for him off under his
  feet.

'Flow on, river!'

(*from* Crossing Brooklyn Ferry)

Flow on, river! flow with the flood-tide, and ebb with the
ebb-tide!
Frolic on, crested and scallop-edg'd waves!
Gorgeous clouds of the sunset! drench with your splendor
me, or the men and women generations after me!
Cross from shore to shore, countless crowds of passengers!
Stand up, tall masts of Mannahatta! stand up, beautiful
hills of Brooklyn!
Throb, baffled and curious brain! throw out questions and
answers!
Suspend here and everywhere, eternal float of solution!
Gaze, loving and thirsting eyes, in the house or street or
public assembly!
Sound out, voices of young men! loudly and musically call
me by my nighest name!
Live, old life! play the part that looks back on the actor or
actress!
Play the old role, the role that is great or small according as
one makes it!
Consider, you who peruse me, whether I may not in
unknown ways be looking upon you;
Be firm, rail over the river, to support those who lean idly,
yet haste with the hasting current;
Fly on, sea-birds! fly sideways, or wheel in large circles
high in the air;
Receive the summer sky, you water, and faithfully hold it
till all downcast eyes have time to take it from you!

Diverge, fine spokes of light, from the shape of my head, or
any one's head, in the sunlit water!
Come on, ships from the lower bay! pass up or down,
white-sail'd schooners, sloops, lighters!
Flaunt away, flags of all nations! be duly lower'd at sunset!
Burn high your fires, foundry chimneys! cast black
shadows at nightfall! cast red and yellow light over the
tops of the houses!
Appearances, now or henceforth, indicate what you are,
You necessary film, continue to envelop the soul,
About my body for me, and your body for you, be hung our
divinest aromas,
Thrive, cities – bring your freight, bring your shows, ample
and sufficient rivers,
Expand, being than which none else is perhaps more
spiritual,
Keep your places, objects than which none else is more
lasting.
You have waited, you always wait, you dumb, beautiful
ministers,
We receive you with free sense at last, and are insatiate
henceforward,
Not you any more shall be able to foil us, or withhold
yourselves from us,
We use you, and do not cast you aside – we plant you
permanently within us,
We fathom you not – we love you – there is perfection in
you also,
You furnish your parts toward eternity,
Great or small, you furnish your parts toward the soul.

Weathers

This is the weather the cuckoo likes,
        And so do I;
When showers betumble the chestnut spikes,
        And nestlings fly:
And the little brown nightingale bills his best,
And they sit outside at 'The Travellers' Rest,'
And maids come forth sprig-muslin drest,
And citizens dream of the south and west,
        And so do I.

This is the weather the shepherd shuns,
        And so do I;
When beeches drip in browns and duns,
        And thresh, and ply;
And hill-hid tides throb, throe on throe,
And meadow rivulets overflow,
And drops on gate-bars hang in a row,
And rooks in families homeward go,
        And so do I.

Mariana

With blackest moss the flower-pots
  Were thickly crusted, one and all:
The rusted nails fell from the knots
  That held the peach to the garden-wall.
The broken sheds look'd sad and strange:
  Unlifted was the clinking latch;
  Weeded and worn the ancient thatch
Upon the lonely moated grange.
    She only said, 'My life is dreary,
      He cometh not,' she said;
    She said, 'I am aweary, aweary,
      I would that I were dead!'

Her tears fell with the dews at even;
  Her tears fell ere the dews were dried;
She could not look on the sweet heaven,
  Either at morn or eventide.
After the flitting of the bats,
  When thickest dark did trance the sky,
  She drew her casement-curtain by,
And glanced athwart the glooming flats.
    She only said, 'The night is dreary,
      He cometh not,' she said;
    She said, 'I am aweary, aweary,
      I would that I were dead!'

Upon the middle of the night,
  Waking she heard the night-fowl crow:
The cock sung out an hour ere light:
  From the dark fen the oxen's low

Came to her: without hope of change,
In sleep she seem'd to walk forlorn,
Till cold winds woke the gray-eyed morn
About the lonely moated grange.
She only said, 'The day is dreary,
He cometh not,' she said;
She said, 'I am aweary, aweary,
I would that I were dead!'

About a stone-cast from the wall
A sluice with blacken'd waters slept,
And o'er it many, round and small,
The cluster'd marish-mosses crept.
Hard by a poplar shook alway,
All silver-green with gnarled bark:
For leagues no other tree did mark
The level waste, the rounding gray.
She only said, 'The day is dreary,
He cometh not,' she said;
She said, 'I am aweary, aweary,
I would that I were dead!'

And ever when the moon was low,
And the shrill winds were up and away,
In the white curtain, to and fro,
She saw the gusty shadow sway.
But when the moon was very low,
And wild winds bound within their cell,
The shadow of the poplar fell
Upon her bed, across her brow.
She only said, 'The night is dreary,
He cometh not,' she said;
She said, 'I am aweary, aweary,
I would that I were dead!'

All day within the dreamy house,
  The doors upon their hinges creak'd;
The blue fly sung in the pane; the mouse
  Behind the mouldering wainscot shriek'd,
Or from the crevice peer'd about.
  Old faces glimmer'd thro' the doors,
  Old footsteps trod the upper floors,
Old voices called her from without.
    She only said, 'The day is dreary,
      He cometh not,' she said;
    She said, 'I am aweary, aweary,
      I would that I were dead!'

The sparrow's chirrup on the roof,
  The slow clock ticking, and the sound
Which to the wooing wind aloof
  The poplar made, did all confound
Her sense; but most she loathed the hour
  When the thick-moted sunbeam lay
  Athwart the chambers, and the day
Was sloping toward his western bower.
    Then, said she, 'I am very dreary,
      He will not come,' she said;
    She wept, 'I am aweary, aweary,
      Oh God, that I were dead!'

The Garden of Love

I went to the Garden of Love,
And saw what I never had seen:
A Chapel was built in the midst,
Where I used to play on the green.

And the gates of this Chapel were shut,
And 'Thou shalt not' writ over the door;
So I turn'd to the Garden of Love
That so many sweet flowers bore;

And I saw it was filled with graves,
And tomb-stones where flowers should be;
And Priests in black gowns were walking their rounds,
And binding with briars my joys & desires.

ANNA WICKHAM

The Fired Pot

In our town, people live in rows.
The only irregular thing in a street is the steeple;
And where that points to, God only knows,
And not the poor disciplined people!

And I have watched the women growing old,
Passionate about pins, and pence, and soap,
Till the heart within my wedded breast grew cold,
And I lost hope.

But a young soldier came to our town,
He spoke his mind most candidly.
He asked me quickly to lie down,
And that was very good for me.

For though I gave him no embrace –
Remembering my duty –
He altered the expression of my face,
And gave me back my beauty.

'Still to be neat, still to be dressed'

Still to be neat, still to be dressed,
As you were going to a feast;
Still to be powdered, still perfumed:
Lady, it is to be presumed,
Though art's hid causes are not found,
All is not sweet, all is not sound.

Give me a look, give me a face,
That makes simplicity a grace;
Robes loosely flowing, hair as free:
Such sweet neglect more taketh me
Than all th' adulteries of art;
They strike mine eyes, but not my heart.

Love in a Life

Room after room,
I hunt the house through
We inhabit together.
Heart, fear nothing, for, heart, thou shalt find her –
Next time, herself! – not the trouble behind her
Left in the curtain, the couch's perfume!
As she brushed it, the cornice-wreath blossomed anew:
Yon looking-glass gleamed at the wave of her feather.

Yet the day wears,
And door succeeds door;
I try the fresh fortune –
Range the wide house from the wing to the centre.
Still the same chance! she goes out as I enter.
Spend my whole day in the quest, – who cares?
But 't is twilight, you see, – with such suites to explore,
Such closets to search, such alcoves to importune!

RICHARD LOVELACE

La Bella Bona Roba

I cannot tell who loves the skeleton
Of a poor marmoset, nought but bone, bone.
Give me a nakedness with her clothes on.

Such whose white-satin upper coat of skin,
Cut upon velvet rich incarnadine,
Has yet a body (and of flesh) within.

Sure it is meant good husbandry in men,
Who do incorporate with aery lean,
T' repair their sides, and get their rib again.

Hard hap unto the huntsman that decrees
Fat joys for all his sweat, when as he sees,
After his 'say, nought but his keeper's fees.

Then Love I beg, when next thou tak'st thy bow,
Thy angry shafts, and dost heart-chasing go,
Pass rascal deer, strike me the largest doe.

CAROL ANN DUFFY

Stuffed

I put two yellow peepers in an owl.
Wow. I fix the grin of Crocodile.
Spiv. I sew the slither of an eel.

I jerk, kick-start, the back hooves of a mule.
Wild. I hold a red rag to a bull.
Mad. I spread the feathers of a gull.

I screw a tight snarl to a weasel.
Fierce. I stitch the flippers on a seal.
Splayed. I pierce the heartbeat of a quail.

I like her to be naked and to kneel.
Tame. My motionless, my living doll.
Mute. And afterwards I like her not to tell.

WILLIAM SHAKESPEARE

The Phoenix and the Turtle

Let the bird of loudest lay,
On the sole Arabian tree,
Herald sad and trumpet be,
To whose sound chaste wings obey.

But thou shrieking harbinger,
Foul precurrer of the fiend,
Augur of the fever's end,
To this troop come thou not near.

From this session interdict
Every fowl of tyrant wing,
Save the eagle, feather'd king:
Keep the obsequy so strict.

Let the priest in surplice white
That defunctive music can,
Be the death-divining swan,
Lest the requiem lack his right.

And thou treble-dated crow,
That thy sable gender mak'st
With the breath thou giv'st and tak'st,
'Mongst our mourners shalt thou go.

Here the anthem doth commence:
Love and constancy is dead;
Phoenix and the turtle fled
In a mutual flame from hence.

So they lov'd, as love in twain
Had the essence but in one;
Two distincts, division none:
Number there in love was slain.

Hearts remote, yet not asunder;
Distance, and no space was seen
'Twixt the turtle and his queen:
But in them it were a wonder.

So between them love did shine,
That the turtle saw his right
Flaming in the phoenix' sight;
Either was the other's mine.

Property was thus appall'd,
That the self was not the same;
Single nature's double name
Neither two nor one was call'd.

Reason, in itself confounded,
Saw division grow together;
To themselves yet either neither,
Simple were so well compounded,

That it cried, 'How true a twain
Seemeth this concordant one!
Love hath reason, reason none,
If what parts can so remain.'

Whereupon it made this threne
To the phoenix and the dove,
Co-supremes and stars of love,
As chorus to their tragic scene.

THRENOS

Beauty, truth, and rarity
Grace in all simplicity,
Here enclos'd in cinders lie.

Death is now the phoenix' nest;
And the turtle's loyal breast
To eternity doth rest,

Leaving no posterity:
'Twas not their infirmity,
It was married chastity.

Truth may seem, but cannot be;
Beauty brag, but 'tis not she;
Truth and beauty buried be.

The Apparition

When by thy scorn, O murd'ress, I am dead,
And that thou think'st thee free
Of all solicitation from me,
Then shall my ghost come to thy bed,
And thee, feigned vestal, in worse arms shall see;
Then thy sick taper will begin to wink,
And he, whose thou art, being tired before,
Will if thou stir, or pinch to wake him, think
    Thou call'st for more,
And in false sleep will from thee shrink,
And then, poor aspen wretch, neglected thou,
Bathed in a cold quicksilver sweat, wilt lie
    A verier ghost than I;
What I will say, I will not tell thee now,
Lest that preserve thee; and since my love is spent,
I'd rather thou should'st painfully repent,
    Than by my threat'nings rest still innocent.

'Her strong enchantments failing'

Her strong enchantments failing,
  Her towers of fear in wreck,
Her limbecks dried of poisons
  And the knife at her neck,

The Queen of air and darkness
  Begins to shrill and cry,
'O young man, O my slayer,
  To-morrow you shall die.'

O Queen of air and darkness,
  I think 'tis truth you say,
And I shall die to-morrow;
  But you will die to-day.

Nursery Rhyme of Innocence and Experience

I had a silver penny
  And an apricot tree
And I said to the sailor
  On the white quay

'Sailor O sailor
  Will you bring me
If I give you my penny
  And my apricot tree

'A fez from Algeria
  An Arab drum to beat
A little gilt sword
  And a parakeet?'

And he smiled and he kissed me
  As strong as death
And I saw his red tongue
  And I felt his sweet breath

'You may keep your penny
  And your apricot tree
And I'll bring your presents
  Back from sea.'

O, the ship dipped down
  On the rim of the sky
And I waited while three
  Long summers went by

Then one steel morning
  On the white quay
I saw a grey ship
  Come in from sea

Slowly she came
  Across the bay
For her flashing rigging
  Was shot away

All round her wake
  The seabirds cried
And flew in and out
  Of the hole in her side

Slowly she came
  In the path of the sun
And I heard the sound
  Of a distant gun

And a stranger came running
  Up to me
From the deck of the ship
  And he said, said he

'O are you the boy
  Who would wait on the quay
With the silver penny
  And the apricot tree?

'I've a plum-coloured fez
  And a drum for thee
And a sword and a parakeet
  From over the sea.'

'O where is the sailor
   With bold red hair?
And what is that volley
   On the bright air?

'O where are the other
   Girls and boys?
And why have you brought me
   Children's toys?'

'Proud Maisie is in the wood'

Proud Maisie is in the wood,
  Walking so early;
Sweet Robin sits on the bush,
  Singing so rarely.

'Tell me, thou bonny bird,
  When shall I marry me?'
'When six braw gentlemen
  Kirkward shall carry ye.'

'Who makes the bridal bed,
  Birdie, say truly?'
'The grey-headed sexton
  That delves the grave duly.'

'The glowworm o'er grave and stone
  Shall light thee steady;
The owl from the steeple sing
  Welcome, proud lady.'

ANONYMOUS

The Twa Corbies

As I was walking all alane,
I heard twa corbies making a mane:
The tane unto the tither did say,
'Whar sall we gang and dine the day?'

'In behint yon auld fail dyke
I wot there lies a new-slain knight;
And naebody kens that he lies there
But his hawk, his hound, and his lady fair.

His hound is to the hunting gane,
His hawk to fetch the wild-fowl hame,
His lady's ta'en anither mate,
So we may mak' our dinner sweet.

Ye'll sit on his white hause-bane,
And I'll pike out his bonny e'en:
Wi' ae lock o' his gowden hair
We'll theek our nest when it grows bare.

Many a one for him maks mane,
But nane shall ken whar he is gane:
O'er his white banes, when they are bare,
The wind sall blaw for evermair.'

corbies: ravens; *fail*: turf; *hause-bane*: collar-bone; *theek*: thatch

La Belle Dame sans Merci

O what can ail thee, knight-at-arms,
  Alone and palely loitering?
The sedge has withered from the lake,
  And no birds sing.

O what can ail thee, knight-at-arms,
  So haggard and so woe-begone?
The squirrel's granary is full,
  And the harvest's done.

I see a lily on thy brow,
  With anguish moist and fever-dew,
And on thy cheeks a fading rose
  Fast withereth too.

I met a lady in the meads,
  Full beautiful – a faery's child,
Her hair was long, her foot was light,
  And her eyes were wild.

I made a garland for her head,
  And bracelets too, and fragrant zone;
She looked at me as she did love,
  And made sweet moan.

I set her on my pacing steed,
  And nothing else saw all day long,
For sidelong would she bend, and sing
  A faery's song.

She found me roots of relish sweet,
And honey wild, and manna-dew,
And sure in language strange she said –
'I love thee true'.

She took me to her elfin grot,
And there she wept and sighed full sore,
And there I shut her wild wild eyes
With kisses four.

And there she lullèd me asleep
And there I dreamed – Ah! woe betide! –
The latest dream I ever dreamt
On the cold hill side.

I saw pale kings and princes too,
Pale warriors, death-pale were they all;
They cried – 'La Belle Dame sans Merci
Thee hath in thrall!'

I saw their starved lips in the gloam,
With horrid warning gapèd wide,
And I awoke and found me here,
On the cold hill's side.

And this is why I sojourn here
Alone and palely loitering,
Though the sedge is withered from the lake,
And no birds sing.

The Phantom Horsewoman

Queer are the ways of a man I know:
He comes and stands
In a careworn craze,
And looks at the sands
And the seaward haze
With moveless hands
And face and gaze,
Then turns to go . . .
And what does he see when he gazes so?

They say he sees as an instant thing
More clear than to-day,
A sweet soft scene
That was once in play
By that briny green;
Yes, notes alway
Warm, real, and keen,
What his back years bring –
A phantom of his own figuring.

Of this vision of his they might say more:
Not only there
Does he see this sight,
But everywhere
In his brain – day, night,
As if on the air
It were drawn rose-bright –
Yea, far from that shore
Does he carry this vision of heretofore:

A ghost-girl-rider. And though, toil-tried,
He withers daily,
Time touches her not,
But she still rides gaily
In his rapt thought
On that shagged and shaly
Atlantic spot,
And as when first eyed
Draws rein and sings to the swing of the tide.

WALTER DE LA MARE

The Listeners

'Is there anybody there?' said the Traveller,
Knocking on the moonlit door;
And his horse in the silence champed the grasses
Of the forest's ferny floor:
And a bird flew up out of the turret,
Above the Traveller's head:
And he smote upon the door again a second time;
'Is there anybody there?' he said.
But no one descended to the Traveller;
No head from the leaf-fringed sill
Leaned over and looked into his grey eyes,
Where he stood perplexed and still.
But only a host of phantom listeners
That dwelt in the lone house then
Stood listening in the quiet of the moonlight
To that voice from the world of men:
Stood thronging the faint moonbeams on the dark stair,
That goes down to the empty hall,
Hearkening in an air stirred and shaken
By the lonely Traveller's call.
And he felt in his heart their strangeness,
Their stillness answering his cry,
While his horse moved, cropping the dark turf,
'Neath the starred and leafy sky;
For he suddenly smote on the door, even
Louder, and lifted his head: –
'Tell them I came, and no one answered,
That I kept my word,' he said.

Never the least stir made the listeners,
    Though every word he spake
Fell echoing through the shadowiness of the still house
    From the one man left awake:
Ay, they heard his foot upon the stirrup,
    And the sound of iron on stone,
And how the silence surged softly backward,
    When the plunging hoofs were gone.

Merlin

O Merlin in your crystal cave
Deep in the diamond of the day,
Will there ever be a singer
Whose music will smooth away
The furrow drawn by Adam's finger
Across the meadow and the wave?
Or a runner who'll outrun
Man's long shadow driving on,
Break through the gate of memory
And hang the apple on the tree?
Will your magic ever show
The sleeping bride shut in her bower,
The day wreathed in its mound of snow
And Time locked in his tower?

'Batter my heart, three-personed God'

Batter my heart, three-personed God, for you
As yet but knock, breathe, shine, and seek to mend;
That I may rise and stand, o'erthrow me and bend
Your force to break, blow, burn, and make me new.
I, like an usurped town to another due,
Labour to admit you, but O, to no end.
Reason, your viceroy in me, me should defend,
But is captived and proves weak or untrue.
Yet dearly I love you and would be loved fain,
But am betrothed unto your enemy.
Divorce me, untie, or break that knot again,
Take me to you, imprison me, for I,
Except you enthrall me, never shall be free,
Nor ever chaste except you ravish me.

The Collar

I struck the board, and cried, 'No more!
I will abroad.
What? shall I ever sigh and pine?
My lines and life are free; free as the road,
Loose as the wind, as large as store.
Shall I be still in suit?
Have I no harvest but a thorn
To let me blood, and not restore
What I have lost with cordial fruit?
Sure there was wine
Before my sighs did dry it: there was corn
Before my tears did drown it.
Is the year only lost to me?
Have I no bays to crown it?
No flowers, no garlands gay? all blasted?
All wasted?
Not so, my heart: but there is fruit,
And thou hast hands.
Recover all thy sigh-blown age
On double pleasures; leave thy cold dispute
Of what is fit, and not. Forsake thy cage,
Thy rope of sands,
Which petty thoughts have made, and made to thee
Good cable, to enforce and draw,
And be thy law,
While thou didst wink and wouldst not see.
Away; take heed:
I will abroad.

Call in thy death's head there: tie up thy fears.
He that forbears
To suit and serve his need,
Deserves his load.'
But as I raved and grew more fierce and wild
At every word,
Methoughts I heard one calling, 'Child!'
And I replied, 'My Lord'.

On My First Son

Farewell, thou child of my right hand, and joy!
My sin was too much hope of thee, loved boy;
Seven years thou wert lent to me, and I thee pay,
Exacted by thy fate, on the just day.
Oh, could I lose all father now! For why
Will man lament the state he should envỳ –
To have so soon 'scaped world's and flesh's rage,
And, if no other misery, yet age?
Rest in soft peace, and, asked, say here doth lie
Ben Jonson his best piece of poetry:
For whose sake, henceforth, all his vows be such
As what he loves may never like too much.

Empty Vessel

I met ayont the cairney
A lass wi' tousie hair
Singin' till a bairnie
That was nae langer there.

Wunds wi' warlds to swing
Dinna sing sae sweet.
The licht that bends owre a' thing
Is less ta'en up wi't.

ayont the cairney: beyond the little cairn

The Emperor of Ice-Cream

Call the roller of big cigars,
The muscular one, and bid him whip
In kitchen cups concupiscent curds.
Let the wenches dawdle in such dress
As they are used to wear, and let the boys
Bring flowers in last month's newspapers.
Let be be final of seem.
The only emperor is the emperor of ice-cream.

Take from the dresser of deal,
Lacking the three glass knobs, that sheet
On which she embroidered fantails once
And spread it so as to cover her face.
If her horny feet protrude, they come
To show how cold she is, and dumb.
Let the lamp affix its beam.
The only emperor is the emperor of ice-cream.

Passing the Graveyard

I see you did not try to save
The bouquet of white flowers I gave;
So fast they wither on your grave.

Why does it hurt the heart to think
Of that most bitter abrupt brink
Where the low-shouldered coffins sink?

These living bodies that we wear
So change by every seventh year
That in a new dress we appear;

Limbs, spongy brain and slogging heart,
No part remains the selfsame part;
Like streams they stay and still depart.

You slipped slow bodies in the past;
Then why should we be so aghast
You flung off the whole flesh at last?

Let him who loves you think instead
That like a woman who has wed
You undressed first and went to bed.

The Childless Father

'Up, Timothy, up with your staff and away!
Not a soul in the village this morning will stay:
The hare has just started from Hamilton's grounds,
And Skiddaw is glad with the cry of the hounds.'

Of coats and of jackets, grey, scarlet, and green,
On the slopes of the pastures all colours were seen;
With their comely blue aprons and caps white as snow,
The girls on the hills make a holiday show.

Fresh sprigs of green box-wood, not six months before,
Fill'd the funeral basin at Timothy's door;
A coffin through Timothy's threshold had past;
One Child did it bear, and that Child was his last.

Now fast up the dell came the noise and the fray,
The horse and the horn, and the hark! hark! away!
Old Timothy took up his staff, and he shut,
With a leisurely motion, the door of his hut.

Perhaps to himself at that moment he said;
'The key I must take, for my Ellen is dead.'
But of this, in my ears, not a word did he speak;
And he went to the chase with a tear on his cheek.

WILLIAM COWPER

The Poplar-Field

The poplars are felled; farewell to the shade
And the whispering sound of the cool colonnade;
The winds play no longer and sing in the leaves,
Nor Ouse on his bosom their image receives.

Twelve years have elapsed since I first took a view
Of my favourite field, and the bank where they grew;
And now in the grass behold they are laid,
And the tree is my seat that once lent me a shade.

The blackbird has fled to another retreat
Where the hazels afford him a screen from the heat,
And the scene where his melody charmed me before
Resounds with his sweet-flowing ditty no more.

My fugitive years are all hasting away,
And I must ere long lie as lowly as they
With a turf on my breast, and a stone at my head,
Ere another such grove shall arise in its stead.

'Tis a sight to engage me, if anything can,
To muse on the perishing pleasures of man;
Though his life be a dream, his enjoyments, I see,
Have a being less durable even than he.

Anthem for Doomed Youth

What passing bells for those who die as cattle?
  Only the monstrous anger of the guns.
  Only the stuttering rifles' rapid rattle
Can patter out their hasty orisons.
No mockeries for them from prayers or bells,
  Nor any voice of mourning save the choirs, –
The shrill, demented choirs of wailing shells;
  And bugles calling for them from sad shires.
What candles may be held to speed them all?
  Not in the hands of boys, but in their eyes
Shall shine the holy glimmers of good-byes.
  The pallor of girls' brows shall be their pall;
Their flowers the tenderness of patient minds,
And each slow dusk a drawing-down of blinds.

'I heard a Fly buzz – when I died'

I heard a Fly buzz – when I died –
The Stillness in the Room
Was like the Stillness in the Air –
Between the Heaves of Storm –

The Eyes around – had wrung them dry –
And Breaths were gathering firm
For that last Onset – when the King
Be witnessed – in the Room –

I willed my Keepsakes – Signed away
What portion of me be
Assignable – and then it was
There interposed a Fly –

With Blue – uncertain stumbling Buzz –
Between the light – and me –
And then the Windows failed – and then
I could not see to see –

JOHN DONNE

'Death, be not proud'

Death, be not proud, though some have called thee
Mighty and dreadful, for thou art not so;
For those whom thou thinkst thou dost overthrow
Die not, poor Death, nor yet canst thou kill me.
From rest and sleep, which but thy pictures be,
Much pleasure – then, from thee much more must flow;
And soonest our best men with thee do go,
Rest of their bones and soul's delivery.
Thou'rt slave to fate, chance, kings, and desperate men,
And dost with poison, war, and sickness dwell;
And poppy or charms can make us sleep as well,
And better than thy stroke. Why swellst thou then?
One short sleep past, we wake eternally,
And death shall be no more. Death, thou shalt die.

'Do not go gentle into that good night'

Do not go gentle into that good night,
Old age should burn and rave at close of day;
Rage, rage against the dying of the light.

Though wise men at their end know dark is right,
Because their words had forked no lightning they
Do not go gentle into that good night.

Good men, the last wave by, crying how bright
Their frail deeds might have danced in a green bay,
Rage, rage against the dying of the light.

Wild men who caught and sang the sun in flight,
And learn, too late, they grieved it on its way,
Do not go gentle into that good night.

Grave men, near death, who see with blinding sight
Blind eyes could blaze like meteors and be gay,
Rage, rage against the dying of the light.

And you, my father, there on the sad height,
Curse, bless, me now with your fierce tears, I pray.
Do not go gentle into that good night.
Rage, rage against the dying of the light.

You're

Clownlike, happiest on your hands,
Feet to the stars, and moon-skulled,
Gilled like a fish. A common-sense
Thumbs-down on the dodo's mode.
Wrapped up in yourself like a spool,
Trawling your dark as owls do.
Mute as a turnip from the Fourth
Of July to All Fools' Day,
O high-riser, my little loaf.

Vague as fog and looked for like mail.
Farther off than Australia.
Bent-backed Atlas, our traveled prawn.
Snug as a bud and at home
Like a sprat in a pickle jug.
A creel of eels, all ripples.
Jumpy as a Mexican bean.
Right, like a well-done sum.
A clean slate, with your own face on.

PAUL MULDOON

The Birth

Seven o'clock. The seventh day of the seventh month of the
  year.
No sooner have I got myself up in lime-green scrubs,
a sterile cap and mask,
and taken my place at the head of the table

than the windlass-women ply their shears
and gralloch-grub
for a footling foot, then, warming to their task,
haul into the inestimable

realm of apple-blossoms and chanterelles and damsons
  and eel-spears
and foxes and the general hubbub
of inkies and jennets and Kickapoos with their lemniscs
or peekaboo-quiffs of Russian sable

and tallow-unctuous vernix, into the realm of the
  widgeon –
the 'whew' or 'yellow-poll', not the 'zuizin' –

Dorothy Aoife Korelitz Muldoon: I watch through floods
  of tears
as they give her a quick rub-a-dub
and whisk
her off to the nursery, then check their staple-guns for
  staples.

Full Moon and Little Frieda

A cool small evening shrunk to a dog bark and the clank of
a bucket –

And you listening.
A spider's web, tense for the dew's touch.
A pail lifted, still and brimming – mirror
To tempt a first star to a tremor.

Cows are going home in the lane there, looping the hedges
with their warm wreaths of breath –
A dark river of blood, many boulders,
Balancing unspilled milk.

'Moon!' you cry suddenly, 'Moon! Moon!'

The moon has stepped back like an artist gazing amazed
at a work
That points at him amazed.

Death of a Naturalist

All year the flax-dam festered in the heart
Of the townland; green and heavy-headed
Flax had rotted there, weighted down by huge sods.
Daily it sweltered in the punishing sun.
Bubbles gargled delicately, bluebottles
Wove a strong gauze of sound around the smell.
There were dragonflies, spotted butterflies,
But best of all was the warm thick slobber
Of frogspawn that grew like clotted water
In the shade of the banks. Here, every spring
I would fill jampotfuls of the jellied
Specks to range on window-sills at home,
On shelves at school, and wait and watch until
The fattening dots burst into nimble-
Swimming tadpoles. Miss Walls would tell us how
The daddy frog was called a bullfrog
And how he croaked and how the mammy frog
Laid hundreds of little eggs and this was
Frogspawn. You could tell the weather by frogs too
For they were yellow in the sun and brown
In rain.

Then one hot day when fields were rank
With cowdung in the grass the angry frogs
Invaded the flax-dam; I ducked through hedges
To a coarse croaking that I had not heard
Before. The air was thick with a bass chorus.
Right down the dam gross-bellied frogs were cocked
On sods; their loose necks pulsed like sails. Some hopped:
The slap and plop were obscene threats. Some sat

Poised like mud grenades, their blunt heads farting.
I sickened, turned, and ran. The great slime kings
Were gathered there for vengeance and I knew
That if I dipped my hand the spawn would clutch it.

'A narrow Fellow in the Grass'

A narrow Fellow in the Grass
Occasionally rides –
You may have met Him – did you not
His notice sudden is –

The Grass divides as with a Comb –
A spotted shaft is seen –
And then it closes at your feet
And opens further on –

He likes a Boggy Acre
A Floor too cool for Corn –
Yet when a Boy, and Barefoot –
I more than once at Noon
Have passed, I thought, a Whip lash
Unbraiding in the Sun
When stooping to secure it
It wrinkled, and was gone –

Several of Nature's People
I know, and they know me –
I feel for them a transport
Of cordiality –

But never met this Fellow
Attended, or alone
Without a tighter breathing
And Zero at the Bone –

Recollections after an Evening Walk

Just as the even bell rung we set out
To wander the fields & the meadows about
& the first thing we markt that was lovly to view
Was the sun hung on nothing & bidding adieu
He seemd like a ball of pure gold in the west
In a cloud like a mountain blue dropping to rest
The clouds all around him were tingd wi his rays
& the trees at a distance seemd all on a blaze
Till lower & lower & sunk from our sight
& blue mist came creeping wi silence & night
The woodman then ceasd wi his hatchet to hack
& bent a way home wi his kid on his back
The mower too lapt up his scythe from our sight
& put on his jacket & bid us good night
The thresher once lumping we heard him no more
He left his barn dust & had shut up his door
The shepherd had told all his sheep in his pen
& hummed his song to his cottage agen
But the sweetest of all seeming music to me
Was the song of the clumbsy brown beetle & bee
The one was a hastning away to his hive
The other was just from his sleeping alive
& our hats he kept knocking as if hed no eyes
& when batterd down he was puzzld to rise
The little gay moth too was lovly to view
A dancing wis liley white wings in the dew
He wiskd oer the water pudge flirting & airy
& perchd on the down headed grass like a fairy
& there came the snail from his shell peeping out

As fear full & cautious as thieves on the rout
The sly jumping frog too had venturd to tramp
& the glow worm had just gun to light up his lamp
To sip of the dew the worm pep[t] from his den
But dreading our footsteps soon vanishd agen
& numbers of creatures apeard in our sight
That live in the silence & sweetness of night
Climbing up the tall grasses or scaling the bough
But these were all namless unoticd till now
& then we wound round neath the brooks willow row
& lookt at the clouds that kept passing below
The moons image too in the brook we could seet
As if twas the tother world under our feet
& we listnd well pleasd at the guggles & groans
The water made passing the pebbles & stones
& then we turnd up by the rut rifted lane
& sought for our cot & the village again
For night gatherd round & shut all from the eye
& a black sutty cloud crept all over the sky
The wet bush we past soon as touchd it woud drop
& the grass neath our feet was as wet as a mop
& as to the town we aproachd very fast
The bat even popt in our face as he past
& the crickets sung loud as we went by the house
& by the barn side we saw many a mouse
Quirking round for the kernels that litterd about
As shook from the straw which the thresher hurld out
& then we came up to our cottage once more
& shut out the night dew & lockt up the door
The dog barkd a welcome well pleasd at our sight
& the owl oer our cot flew & woopt a good night

Dover Beach

The sea is calm to-night,
The tide is full, the moon lies fair
Upon the Straits; – on the French coast, the light
Gleams, and is gone; the cliffs of England stand,
Glimmering and vast, out in the tranquil bay.
Come to the window, sweet is the night air!
Only, from the long line of spray
Where the ebb meets the moon-blanch'd sand,
Listen! you hear the grating roar
Of pebbles which the waves suck back, and fling,
At their return, up the high strand,
Begin, and cease, and then again begin,
With tremulous cadence slow, and bring
The eternal note of sadness in.

Sophocles long ago
Heard it on the Aegaean, and it brought
Into his mind the turbid ebb and flow
Of human misery; we
Find also in the sound a thought,
Hearing it by this distant northern sea.

The sea of faith
Was once, too, at the full, and round earth's shore
Lay like the folds of a bright girdle furl'd;
But now I only hear
Its melancholy, long, withdrawing roar,
Retreating to the breath
Of the night-wind down the vast edges drear
And naked shingles of the world.

Ah, love, let us be true
To one another! for the world, which seems
To lie before us like a land of dreams,
So various, so beautiful, so new,
Hath really neither joy, nor love, nor light,
Nor certitude, nor peace, nor help for pain;
And we are here as on a darkling plain
Swept with confused alarms of struggle and flight,
Where ignorant armies clash by night.

W. H. AUDEN

Lullaby

Lay your sleeping head, my love,
Human on my faithless arm;
Time and fevers burn away
Individual beauty from
Thoughtful children, and the grave
Proves the child ephemeral:
But in my arms till break of day
Let the living creature lie,
Mortal, guilty, but to me
The entirely beautiful.

Soul and body have no bounds:
To lovers as they lie upon
Her tolerant enchanted slope
In their ordinary swoon,
Grave the vision Venus sends
Of supernatural sympathy,
Universal love and hope;
While an abstract insight wakes
Among the glaciers and the rocks
The hermit's carnal ecstasy.

Certainty, fidelity
On the stroke of midnight pass
Like vibrations of a bell
And fashionable madmen raise
Their pedantic boring cry:
Every farthing of the cost,
All the dreaded cards foretell,
Shall be paid, but from this night

Not a whisper, not a thought,
Not a kiss nor look be lost.

Beauty, midnight, vision dies:
Let the winds of dawn that blow
Softly round your dreaming head
Such a day of welcome show
Eye and knocking heart may bless,
Find our mortal world enough;
Noons of dryness find you fed
By the involuntary powers,
Nights of insult let you pass
Watched by every human love.

To His Coy Mistress

Had we but world enough, and time,
This coyness Lady were no crime.
We would sit down, and think which way
To walk, and pass our long love's day.
Thou by the Indian Ganges' side
Should'st rubies find: I by the tide
Of Humber would complain. I would
Love you ten years before the Flood:
And you should, if you please, refuse
Till the conversion of the Jews.
My vegetable love should grow
Vaster then empires, and more slow.
An hundred years should go to praise
Thine eyes, and on thy forehead gaze;
Two hundred to adore each breast,
But thirty thousand to the rest;
An age at least to every part,
And the last age should show your heart.
For, lady, you deserve this state;
Nor would I love at lower rate.
But at my back I always hear
Time's wingèd chariot hurrying near;
And yonder all before us lie
Deserts of vast eternity.
Thy beauty shall no more be found;
Nor, in thy marble vault, shall sound
My echoing song; then worms shall try
That long-preserv'd virginity,
And your quaint honour turn to dust,

And into ashes all my lust.
The grave's a fine and private place,
But none, I think, do there embrace.
  Now therefore, while the youthful hue
Sits on thy skin like morning dew,
And while thy willing soul transpires
At every pore with instant fires,
Now let us sport us while we may;
And now, like am'rous birds of prey,
Rather at once our time devour,
Than languish in his slow-chapped power.
Let us roll all our strength, and all
Our sweetness, up into one ball,
And tear our pleasures with rough strife
Thorough the iron gates of life.
Thus, though we cannot make our sun
Stand still, yet we will make him run.

Dinner with My Mother

My mother is saying 'Now'.
'Now,' she says, taking down a saucepan,
putting it on the stove.
She doesn't say anything else for a while,

so that time passes slowly, on the simmer,
until it is 'Now' again
as she hammers out our steaks
for Steak Diane.

I have to be on hand at times like this
for table-laying,
drink replenishment
and general conversational encouragement,

but I am getting hungry
and there is nowhere to sit down.
'Now,' I say, making a point
of opening a bottle of wine.

My mother isn't listening.
She's miles away,
testing the sauce with a spoon,
narrowing her eyes through the steam.

'Now,' she says very slowly, meaning
which is it to be,
the rosemary or tarragon vinegar
for the salad dressing?

I hold my breath, lest anything
should go wrong at the last minute.
But now it is really 'Now',
our time to sit and eat.

TED HUGHES

The Thought-Fox

I imagine this midnight moment's forest:
Something else is alive
Beside the clock's loneliness
And this blank page where my fingers move.

Through the window I see no star:
Something more near
Though deeper within darkness
Is entering the loneliness:

Cold, delicately as the dark snow
A fox's nose touches twig, leaf;
Two eyes serve a movement, that now
And again now, and now, and now

Sets neat prints into the snow
Between trees, and warily a lame
Shadow lags by stump and in hollow
Of a body that is bold to come

Across clearings, an eye,
A widening deepening greenness,
Brilliantly, concentratedly,
Coming about its own business

Till, with a sudden sharp hot stink of fox
It enters the dark hole of the head.
The window is starless still; the clock ticks,
The page is printed.

'As kingfishers catch fire'

As kingfishers catch fire, dragonflies draw flame;
  As tumbled over rim in roundy wells
  Stones ring; like each tucked string tells, each hung bell's
Bow swung finds tongue to fling out broad its name;
Each mortal thing does one thing and the same:
  Deals out that being indoors each one dwells;
  Selves – goes itself; *myself* it speaks and spells,
Crying *What I do is me: for that I came.*

Í say more: the just man justices;
  Keeps gráce: thát keeps all his goings graces;
Acts in God's eye what in God's eye he is –
  Chríst. For Christ plays in ten thousand places,
Lovely in limbs, and lovely in eyes not his
  To the Father through the features of men's faces.

SEAMUS HEANEY

Anahorish

My 'place of clear water',
the first hill in the world
where springs washed into
the shiny grass

and darkened cobbles
in the bed of the lane.
Anahorish, soft gradient
of consonant, vowel-meadow,

after-image of lamps
swung through the yards
on winter evenings.
With pails and barrows

those mound-dwellers
go waist-deep in mist
to break the light ice
at wells and dunghills.

WALLACE STEVENS

Nomad Exquisite

As the immense dew of Florida
Brings forth
The big-finned palm
And green vine angering for life,

As the immense dew of Florida
Brings forth hymn and hymn
From the beholder,
Beholding all these green sides
And gold sides of green sides,

And blessed mornings,
Meet for the eye of the young alligator,
And lightning colors
So, in me, come flinging
Forms, flames, and the flakes of flames.

To His Son

Three things there be that prosper up apace
And flourish, whilst they grow asunder far,
But on a day they meet all in one place,
And when they meet, they one another mar;
And they be these, the wood, the weed, the wag.
The wood is that which makes the Gallow-tree,
The weed is that which strings the Hangman's bag,
The wag, my pretty knave, betokeneth thee.
Mark well, dear boy, whilst these assemble not,
Green springs the tree, hemp grows, the wag is wild,
But when they meet, it makes the timber rot,
It frets the halter, and it chokes the child.
Then bless thee, and beware, and let us pray,
We part not with thee at this meeting day.

'Thrice toss these oaken ashes in the air'

Thrice toss these oaken ashes in the air,
Thrice sit thou mute in this enchanted chair;
Then thrice-three times tie up this true love's knot,
And murmur soft 'She will or she will not.'

Go burn these poisonous weeds in yon blue fire,
These screech-owl's feathers and this prickling brier,
This cypress gathered at a dead man's grave,
That all thy fears and cares an end may have.

Then come, you Fairies! dance with me a round!
Melt her hard heart with your melodious sound! –
In vain are all the charms I can devise:
She hath an art to break them with her eyes.

My Cats

I like to toss him up and down
A heavy cat weighs half a Crown
With a hey do diddle my cat Brown.

I like to pinch him on the sly
When nobody is passing by
With a hey do diddle my cat Fry.

I like to ruffle up his pride
And watch him skip and turn aside
With a hey do diddle my cat Hyde.

Hey Brown and Fry and Hyde my cats
That sit on tombstone for your mats.

Our Bias

The hour-glass whispers to the lion's roar,
The clock-towers tell the gardens day and night
How many errors Time has patience for,
How wrong they are in being always right.

Yet Time, however loud its chimes or deep,
However fast its falling torrent flows,
Has never put one lion off his leap
Nor shaken the assurance of a rose.

For they, it seems, care only for success:
While we choose words according to their sound
And judge a problem by its awkwardness;

And Time with us was always popular.
When have we not preferred some going round
To going straight to where we are?

'Like as the waves make towards the pebbled shore'

Like as the waves make towards the pebbled shore,
So do our minutes hasten to their end;
Each changing place with that which goes before,
In sequent toil all forwards do contend.
Nativity, once in the main of light,
Crawls to maturity, wherewith being crown'd,
Crooked eclipses 'gainst his glory fight,
And Time that gave doth now his gift confound.
Time doth transfix the flourish set on youth
And delves the parallels in beauty's brow,
Feeds on the rarities of nature's truth,
And nothing stands but for his scythe to mow:
  And yet to times in hope my verse shall stand,
  Praising thy worth, despite his cruel hand

Remember

Remember me when I am gone away,
  Gone far away into the silent land;
  When you can no more hold me by the hand,
Nor I half turn to go yet turning stay.
Remember me when no more day by day
  You tell me of our future that you planned:
  Only remember me; you understand
It will be late to counsel then or pray.
Yet if you should forget me for a while
  And afterwards remember, do not grieve:
  For if the darkness and corruption leave
  A vestige of the thoughts that once I had,
Better by far you should forget and smile
  Than that you should remember and be sad.

LOUIS MACNEICE

The Sunlight on the Garden

The sunlight on the garden
Hardens and grows cold,
We cannot cage the minute
Within its nets of gold,
When all is told
We cannot beg for pardon.

Our freedom as free lances
Advances towards its end;
The earth compels, upon it
Sonnets and birds descend;
And soon, my friend,
We shall have no time for dances.

The sky was good for flying
Defying the church bells
And every evil iron
Siren and what it tells:
The earth compels,
We are dying, Egypt, dying

And not expecting pardon,
Hardened in heart anew,
But glad to have sat under
Thunder and rain with you,
And grateful too
For sunlight on the garden.

WENDY COPE

In the Rhine Valley

Die Farben der Bäume sind schön
And the sky's and the river's blue-greys
And the *Burg*, almost lost in the haze.

You're patient. You help me to learn
And you smile as I practise the phrase,
'Die Farben der Bäume sind schön.'

October. The year's on the turn –
It will take us our separate ways
But the sun shines. And we have two days.
Die Farben der Bäume sind schön.

Die Farben der Bäume sind schön: the colours of the trees are beautiful;
Burg: castle

LEIGH HUNT

'Jenny kiss'd me when we met'

Jenny kiss'd me when we met,
  Jumping from the chair she sat in;
Time, you thief, who love to get
  Sweets into your list, put that in!
Say I'm weary, say I'm sad,
  Say that health and wealth have miss'd me,
Say I'm growing old, but add,
    Jenny kiss'd me.

GEORGE GORDON, LORD BYRON

'So, we'll go no more a-roving'

So, we'll go no more a-roving
  So late into the night,
Though the heart be still as loving
  And the moon be still as bright.

For the sword outwears its sheath,
  And the soul wears out the breast,
And the heart must pause to breathe,
  And love itself have rest.

Though the night was made for loving,
  And the day returns too soon,
Yet we'll go no more a-roving
  By the light of the moon.

'Fall, leaves, fall'

Fall, leaves, fall; die, flowers, away;
Lengthen night and shorten day;
Every leaf speaks bliss to me,
Fluttering from the autumn tree.

I shall smile when wreaths of snow
Blossom where the rose should grow;
I shall sing when night's decay
Ushers in a drearier day.

Sestina

September rain falls on the house.
In the failing light, the old grandmother
sits in the kitchen with the child
beside the Little Marvel Stove,
reading the jokes from the almanac,
laughing and talking to hide her tears.

She thinks that her equinoctial tears
and the rain that beats on the roof of the house
were both foretold by the almanac,
but only known to a grandmother.
The iron kettle sings on the stove.
She cuts some bread and says to the child,

It's time for tea now; but the child
is watching the teakettle's small hard tears
dance like mad on the hot black stove,
the way the rain must dance on the house.
Tidying up, the old grandmother
hangs up the clever almanac

on its string. Birdlike, the almanac
hovers half open above the child,
hovers above the old grandmother
and her teacup full of dark brown tears.
She shivers and says she thinks the house
feels chilly, and puts more wood in the stove.

It was to be, says the Marvel Stove.
I know what I know, says the almanac.
With crayons the child draws a rigid house

and a winding pathway. Then the child
puts in a man with buttons like tears
and shows it proudly to the grandmother.

But secretly, while the grandmother
busies herself about the stove,
and little moons fall down like tears
from between the pages of the almanac
into the flower bed the child
has carefully placed in the front of the house.

Time to plant tears, says the almanac.
The grandmother sings to the marvellous stove
and the child draws another inscrutable house.

'After great pain, a formal feeling comes'

After great pain, a formal feeling comes –
The Nerves sit ceremonious, like Tombs –
The stiff Heart questions was it He, that bore,
And Yesterday, or Centuries before?

The Feet, mechanical, go round –
Of Ground, or Air, or Ought –
A Wooden way
Regardless grown,
A Quartz contentment, like a stone –

This is the Hour of Lead –
Remembered, if outlived,
As Freezing persons, recollect the Snow –
First – Chill – then Stupor – then the letting go –

Exposure

Our brains ache, in the merciless iced east winds that knive
us . . .
Wearied we keep awake because the night is silent . . .
Low, drooping flares confuse our memory of the salient . . .
Worried by silence, sentries whisper, curious, nervous,
But nothing happens.

Watching, we hear the mad gusts tugging on the wire,
Like twitching agonies of men among its brambles.
Northward, incessantly, the flickering gunnery rumbles,
Far off, like a dull rumour of some other war.
What are we doing here?

The poignant misery of dawn begins to grow . . .
We only know war lasts, rain soaks, and clouds sag
stormy.
Dawn massing in the east her melancholy army
Attacks once more in ranks on shivering ranks of gray,
But nothing happens.

Sudden successive flights of bullets streak the silence.
Less deadly than the air that shudders black with snow,
With sidelong flowing flakes that flock, pause, and renew,
We watch them wandering up and down the wind's
nonchalance,
But nothing happens.

Pale flakes with fingering stealth come feeling for our
faces –
We cringe in holes, back on forgotten dreams, and stare,
snow-dazed,

Deep into grassier ditches. So we drowse, sun-dozed,
Littered with blossoms trickling where the blackbird
fusses.
Is it that we are dying?

Slowly our ghosts drag home: glimpsing the sunk fires,
glozed
With crusted dark-red jewels; crickets jingle there;
For hours the innocent mice rejoice: the house is theirs;
Shutters and doors, all closed: on us the doors are closed, –
We turn back to our dying.

Since we believe not otherwise can kind fires burn;
Nor ever suns smile true on child, or field, or fruit.
For God's invincible spring our love is made afraid;
Therefore, not loath, we lie out here; therefore were born,
For love of God seems dying.

To-night, His frost will fasten on this mud and us,
Shrivelling many hands, puckering foreheads crisp.
The burying-party, picks and shovels in their shaking
grasp,
Pause over half-known faces. All their eyes are ice,
But nothing happens.

Rain

Rain, midnight rain, nothing but the wild rain
On this bleak hut, and solitude, and me
Remembering again that I shall die
And neither hear the rain nor give it thanks
For washing me cleaner than I have been
Since I was born into this solitude.
Blessed are the dead that the rain rains upon:
But here I pray that none whom once I loved
Is dying to-night or lying still awake
Solitary, listening to the rain,
Either in pain or thus in sympathy
Helpless among the living and the dead,
Like a cold water among broken reeds,
Myriads of broken reeds all still and stiff,
Like me who have no love which this wild rain
Has not dissolved except the love of death,
If love it be for what is perfect and
Cannot, the tempest tells me, disappoint.

SAMUEL TAYLOR COLERIDGE

Frost at Midnight

The frost performs its secret ministry,
Unhelped by any wind. The owlet's cry
Came loud – and hark, again! loud as before.
The inmates of my cottage, all at rest,
Have left me to that solitude, which suits
Abstruser musings: save that at my side
My cradled infant slumbers peacefully.
'Tis calm indeed! so calm, that it disturbs
And vexes meditation with its strange
And extreme silentness. Sea, hill, and wood,
This populous village! Sea, and hill, and wood,
With all the numberless goings on of life,
Inaudible as dreams! the thin blue flame
Lies on my low burnt fire, and quivers not;
Only that film, which fluttered on the grate,
Still flutters there, the sole unquiet thing.
Methinks, its motion in this hush of nature
Gives it dim sympathies with me who live,
Making it a companionable form,
Whose puny flaps and freaks the idling Spirit
By its own moods interprets, every where
Echo or mirror seeking of itself,
And makes a toy of Thought.

But O! how oft,
How oft, at school, with most believing mind,
Presageful, have I gazed upon the bars,
To watch that fluttering stranger! and as oft
With unclosed lids, already had I dreamt
Of my sweet birth-place, and the old church tower

Whose bells, the poor man's only music, rang
From morn to evening, all the hot Fair-day,
So sweetly, that they stirred and haunted me
With a wild pleasure, falling on mine ear
Most like articulate sounds of things to come!
So gazed I, till the soothing things I dreamt
Lulled me to sleep, and sleep prolonged my dreams!
And so I brooded all the following morn,
Awed by the stern preceptor's face, mine eye
Fixed with mock study on my swimming book:
Save if the door half opened, and I snatched
A hasty glance, and still my heart leaped up.
For still I hoped to see the stranger's face,
Townsman, or aunt, or sister more beloved,
My play-mate when we both were clothed alike!

Dear Babe, that sleepest cradled by my side,
Whose gentle breathings, heard in this deep calm,
Fill up the interspersed vacancies
And momentary pauses of the thought!
My babe so beautiful! it thrills my heart
With tender gladness, thus to look at thee,
And think that thou shalt learn far other lore
And in far other scenes! For I was reared
In the great city, pent 'mid cloisters dim,
And saw nought lovely but the sky and stars.
But thou, my babe! shalt wander like a breeze
By lakes and sandy shores, beneath the crags
Of ancient mountain, and beneath the clouds,
Which image in their bulk both lakes and shores
And mountain crags: so shalt thou see and hear
The lovely shapes and sounds intelligible
Of that eternal language, which thy God

Utters, who from eternity doth teach
Himself in all, and all things in himself.
Great universal Teacher! he shall mould
Thy spirit, and by giving make it ask.

Therefore all seasons shall be sweet to thee,
Whether the summer clothe the general earth
With greenness, or the redbreast sit and sing
Betwixt the tufts of snow on the bare branch
Of mossy apple-tree, while the nigh thatch
Smokes in the sun-thaw; whether the eave-drops fall
Heard only in the trances of the blast,
Or if the secret ministry of frost
Shall hang them up in silent icicles,
Quietly shining to the quiet Moon.

'Now winter nights enlarge'

Now winter nights enlarge
The number of their hours,
And clouds their storms discharge
Upon the airy towers.
Let now the chimneys blaze,
And cups o'erflow with wine;
Let well-tuned words amaze
With harmony divine.
Now yellow waxen lights
Shall wait on honey love,
While youthful revels, masques, and courtly sights
Sleep's leaden spells remove.

This time doth well dispense
With lovers' long discourse;
Much speech hath some defence,
Though beauty no remorse.
All do not all things well;
Some measures comely tread,
Some knotted riddles tell,
Some poems smoothly read.
The summer hath his joys
And winter his delights;
Though love and all his pleasures are but toys,
They shorten tedious nights.

DYLAN THOMAS

'In my craft or sullen art'

In my craft or sullen art
Exercised in the still night
When only the moon rages
And the lovers lie abed
With all their griefs in their arms,
I labour by singing light
Not for ambition or bread
Or the strut and trade of charms
On the ivory stages
But for the common wages
Of their most secret heart.

Not for the proud man apart
From the raging moon I write
On these spindrift pages
Nor for the towering dead
With their nightingales and psalms
But for the lovers, their arms
Round the griefs of the ages,
Who pay no praise or wages
Nor heed my craft or art.

I Leave This at Your Ear

I leave this at your ear for when you wake,
A creature in its abstract cage asleep.
Your dreams blindfold you by the light they make.

The owl called from the naked-woman tree
As I came down by the Kyle farm to hear
Your house silent by the speaking sea.

I have come late but I have come before
Later with slaked steps from stone to stone
To hope to find you listening for the door.

I stand in the ticking room. My dear, I take
A moth kiss from your breath. The shore gulls cry.
I leave this at your ear for when you wake.

Notes

page

3 *Kubla Khan* See editor's foreword.

5 *Byzantium* Uniform stanzas, but containing a great variety of line-lengths. Still, very different in effect from the spontaneous-looking progress of 'Kubla Khan'. Note the number of words and phrases repeated or modified by Yeats, within lines or across stanzas.

7 *'The world is too much with us'* Our first sonnet, this one on the Italian model, with a break or turn in the argument between the first eight lines (always rhymed abbaabba) and the last six (in this instance, cdcdcd). Its appeal to so many poets, since the sonnet form was imported into English in the sixteenth century, suggests that it answers a deep need for just such a balance between what might be called the statement of the octave and the answer of the sestet. Wordsworth's regret for the consolations of 'a creed outworn' dies away musically in a series of *h* and *o* sounds.

8 *Bavarian Gentians* Repetition, sometimes to the point of nagging the reader into either submission or exasperated resistance, is the very stuff of both Lawrence's prose and his poetry. In this otherwise unconventionally structured poem, the few end-rhymes seem almost a by-product of his banging-away at a small range of words, names and shared vowel-sounds.

9 *Bermudas* 'With falling oars they kept the time': hard not to see Marvell's tetrameters as the equivalent of oars – paired, stiff but vigorous, and keeping the poem moving dashingly along.

11 *The Bight* Apparently informal, and yet held together and kept lively by a host of repetitions, qualifications and subtle verbal correspondences (key word here). In a letter to another poet, Bishop once wrote defending her avoidance of tradi-

tional iambic metre and suggesting that 'an equally great "cumulative effect" might be built up by a series of irregularities' – as she demonstrates here.

13 *Cargoes* No main verb, just three vivid verbal pictures set off against a stanzaic structure that ambivalently combines conventional metre with chant-like thumping. Although the poem must be as popular as any written in the twentieth century, Masefield has received scant critical credit for the stroke of genius by which he came up with this durable, one-off form.

14 *From a Railway Carriage* Clatter of anapaests, mainly. The model, too, for W. H. Auden's celebrated railway poem, 'Night Mail'?

15 *'When icicles hang by the wall'* One of a pair of songs from *Love's Labour's Lost*. An exemplary list-poem, with rhymes pointing the bleak isolation of each thing or person glimpsed and the ironically 'merry note' of the owl as unifying factor.

16 *'Sweet Suffolk owl, so trimly dight'* From a book of songs collected by Thomas Vautor in 1619. The particularity of '*Suffolk* owl' is as important as the names 'Dick' or 'Marian' in Shakespeare's song.

17 *Adlestrop* Like the preceding piece, in its particularity. Note also the balancing of repeated words and grammatical constructions, both at close quarters and far apart. And what would you say was the effect of having 'mistier', in the final stanza, chime with 'Oxfordshire' before meeting its metrically confirmed rhyme in 'Gloucestershire'?

18 *'Pleasure it is'* Another song. The final repetition may have been dictated by musical expedience, but on the page it has an effect greater than the apparent simplicity of its sentiment.

19 *The Trees* Artfully placed rhymes, assonance and alliteration. Plus – once more – the power of repetition, although in this case the word in question poignantly loses its freshness in the process.

20 *Thistles* First of a run of poems touching – this one in passing, but nonetheless pertinently – on the subject of the poet's own material, words.

21 *Words* Short lines, therefore tight rhymes, underwrite the argument.

23 *The Son* Serious praise of that scorned device, the pun.

24 *The Earthen Lot* From *The School of Eloquence*, a sequence of 16-line poems which its author calls sonnets, possibly after the example of the 16-line poems in George Meredith's *Modern Love* (1862), although their relationship to the 14-line prototype (see notes to pages 7 and 96) would be hard to define. It may be best to regard this as an aspect of Harrison's on-going argument with the English literary tradition, its forms, accepted diction and perceived political attitudes.

25 *Quoof* Closer than Harrison's to the traditional sonnet, in spite of the shortness and metrical unorthodoxy of most of its lines, and its carefully disguised rhyming. My own theory, not corroborated by the author, is that 'quoof' is onomatopoeia for the gasp of steam a hot-water bottle gives out when patted, before the stopper is screwed in.

26 *Clock a Clay* Speaking for the creature, Clare employs his local (Northamptonshire) dialect word and makes a point about the value and precarious survival of such a poetic resource. The small range of rhyme-words may, in the context, be considered a kind of eloquence-in-restraint.

27 *Mushrooms* Again, a poet speaks for the 'Perfectly voiceless'. What the mushrooms are given to say seems squeezed, under pressure, through Plath's narrow stanzas.

29 *To a Mouse* Unlike Clare (see page 26) Burns speaks to, not for, his 'cowrin, tim'rous beastie', and yet dialect is still the preferred means. The stanza he uses is itself a Scottish product, called 'Standard Habbie' from its earliest known occurrence in a poem in praise of the piper Habbie Simson, by Robert Sempill (?1590–?1660).

31 *The Mosquito* 'Monsieur'? So the mosquito must have been French? And a male?

34 *Spider* 'You're your own yoyo, aren't you?' A rhetorical question that answers itself mimetically – what better way of conversing with a spider, or celebrating *its* creative skills?

35 *The Tyger* Indispensable. Even more than the preceding poem, it depends on the rhetorical question for its rapport with the subject. Repetition, too – and not just in the invocation or salutation – is an important device.

36 and 40 *'For I will consider my Cat Jeoffry'* and *Poem* Two widely different approaches to catching the essence of feline nature, one lavish and quasi-biblical in style, the other fastidiously economical. By doing without conventional metre and breaking his lines against even the grain of the syntax, Williams opens up a dialogue between eye and ear that adds new possibilities to twentieth-century versification.

41 *A Toccata of Galuppi's* There is no line here that could not have been broken cleanly in the middle, to give each stanza six lines alternating unrhymed feminine with rhymed masculine endings (if the gender terms are still allowable in differentiating between words with the accent on their final syllable from those accented penultimately or antepenultimately). Browning's actual arrangement, which flies in the face of conventional wisdom that the placing of the caesura, or mid-line pause, should be varied as much as possible throughout the poem, makes his lines seem burdened almost to the point of snapping.

44 *Tarantella* Onomatopoeia, crude and unashamed. And why not?

46 *My Papa's Waltz* Three beats to the line, no doubt in honour of the waltz's three to the bar.

47 *Bagpipe Music* Social comment in the guise of a surreal Scottish romp, with the pipes' drone audible in the inexact rhyming.

49 and 50 *'The splendour falls on castle walls'* and *Heaven* Two uses of echo effect. In Herbert's case, the device allows him to rhyme words which conventional strictures against the pairing of homonyms, or words too like each other, would have forbidden. The impulse to break rules, or at least to test their limits, cannot be separated from the spiritual debate he conducts throughout his work.

51 *A Nocturnal Sketch* The unlikely nature of the challenge Hood sets himself here, and his considerable success in meeting it, deserve a cheer.

53 *Morning in Madrid* Poet as impromptu note-taker, using rhyme to suggest pattern within randomness.

54 *Prelude* As above, with the added piquancy of grammatically correct sentences mixing with verbless ones on the same level, the lucky find of the aural relationship between 'steams' and 'stamps', and the exquisitely placed pause before the final line.

55 *London Snow* What we have here, as regards rhyme-scheme, is *terza rima* – the Italian verse-form perfected by Dante and not often found in English. Meanwhile, a blanket of descriptive words makes anything firmer than the most notional five beats per line impossible to discern.

57 *Hurrahing in Harvest* This Italian sonnet shares its pattern of rhymes with the Wordsworth on page 7, but that is the limit of any resemblance, and even in its rhyming it seems to want to burst all constraints. Yet Hopkins returned to the sonnet form time and time again, as if finding there the ideal structure for his spiritual exercises.

58 *'Flow on, river'* Whitman's exuberance was less tolerant of formal constraint. Even his on-rushing lines, though, benefit from the old stand-bys of repetition and alliteration, both setting the style in the opening flourish to this final section of 'Crossing Brooklyn Ferry'.

60 *Weathers* Repetition, contrast, balance.

61 *Mariana* Amid so much descriptive plushness and metrical aplomb, an unruly line like 'And the shrill winds were up and away' comes like the tantalising hint of fresh air it was no doubt meant to be.

64 *The Garden of Love* Blake's departure, in the last two lines, from his established metrical pattern surprises at each reading.

65 *The Fired Pot* The deliberately dishevelled versification, and ballad-like rhyming of 'candidly' with 'me', are both to the point.

66 *'Still to be neat, still to be dressed'* Metrically, this is one of the most fascinating poems in the language. Written by Jonson as a song for his play *The Silent Woman* (1609), it ostensibly consists of iambic tetrameters, and yet there is hardly a line that, spoken naturally (or sung?), conforms to the pattern. Most disruptive of all, the very first line suggests quite another rhythm, which is taken up identically by lines 6 and 7, while elsewhere the tonal emphasis is often at odds with the metrical foundation. I regard this as the work of a master versifier calling attention to what might be called the 'adulteries' of his own art.

67 *Love in a Life* Ruffled, breathless – a little erotic masterpiece.

68 *La Bella Bona Roba* More salacious, perhaps, than erotic, Lovelace's poem in praise of fat women does not quite sustain the tumbling-over-itself energy of its first few lines. In the fourth stanza, ''say' is short for 'assay', a hunting term meaning estimation of the fatness of a stag.

69 *Stuffed* Rhymed throughout on *l*-sounds and packed tight with menace.

70 *The Phoenix and the Turtle* The last line before the 'Threnos' (lament, or dirge) is the only one to break the strict metrical pattern, and that by the addition of a single syllable. The point may be to announce transition into a different order of utterance. Otherwise, ceremony and severity prevail.

73 *The Apparition* Keeping the versification unsettled throughout, Donne throws in the phrases 'thy sick taper' and 'cold quicksilver sweat', with their sly internal rhyming, to bring home the physical immediacy of his threat.

74 *'Her strong enchantments failing'* 'And the knife at her neck' stands starkly apart from the rest of the poem in relation to its metre – for dramatic reasons that do not need to be spelt out.

75 *'Nursery Rhyme of Innocence and Experience'* A nursery rhyme, perhaps, but enhanced by devices borrowed from the ballad tradition: quatrain verses, repetition and listing, liberal use of 'and', and – above all – direct speech.

78 *'Proud Maisie is in the wood'* This goes beyond antiquarian pastiche, I think, although it was written for a character in one of Scott's historical novels, *Heart of Midlothian* (1818).

79 *The Twa Corbies* The real thing, spare and unembellished.

80 *La Belle Dame sans Merci* A shiver down the spine each time, at line 4.

82 *The Phantom Horsewoman* Here, it's the last line that carries the charge, almost as if it had blown in from a different poetic world.

84 *The Listeners* The alternation of longer and shorter lines is handled with infallible instinct, and, I think, lends the poem its uniquely agitated and unforgettable atmosphere.

86 *Merlin* The basic structure of rhyming couplets looks straightforward, but the centre of gravity wavers from couplet to couplet and the poem is in a state of constant restlessness, as if fretting at the unanswerability of its own questions.

87 and 88 *'Batter my heart, three-personed God'* and *The Collar* Two of the great poems of rebellion or disaffection from, and then submission to, God's authority, each quite distinct in form and (therefore) character: Donne's Italian sonnet bursting at the seams with argument; Herbert's looser structure paradoxically more highly streamlined and reaching its resolution with disconcerting abruptness.

90 *On My First Son* It's the pause, or gulp, enforced by the metre between 'Jonson' and 'his' in line 10 – the light word 'his' falling on the iambic beat – that brings tears to the eyes if you try reading this aloud.

91 *Empty Vessel* The second stanza comments on the first from a slight, delicately calculated, metrical and tonal distance.

92 *The Emperor of Ice-Cream* Gaudy nonsense, as some critics have claimed? Or a heart-breaking poem about the improvised nature of mourning in an ephemeral world?

93 *Passing the Graveyard* It's the lack of connectives – the *ands* and *buts* and *sos* and *fors* of ordinary discourse – that helps to

give these stanzas their heightened quality, as if poised above the void.

94 and 95 *The Childless Father* and *The Poplar-Field* Curious that two poems to do with grieving should share the same jaunty metre. Cowper's gets off to the more hesitant start, with a syllable missing where the semi-colon now stands, and continues more loosely.

96 *Anthem for Doomed Youth* An English sonnet: that is, three quatrains and a couplet to round them off. In place of the change of attack that the Italian form requires just after midway (see note to page 7), there is the measured, three-stage build-up to a resonant conclusion that Owen manages so movingly here.

97 *'I heard a Fly buzz – when I died'* What daring – to attach this equivocal moment to the distracting buzz of a fly! The metaphysical poem vindicated in terms of pure, un-otherwordly sound.

98 *'Death, be not proud'* Another of Donne's Italian sonnets (see page 87), only with the sestet rhymes appearing in a different order. If the argument becomes blustery at that point, the final surge is wholly persuasive.

99 *'Do not go gentle into that good night'* Text-book villanelle, in which Thomas takes none of the liberties that some other twentieth-century villanelle writers have allowed themselves – making small but obtrusive alterations to the wording of repeated lines, for instance. Note the balance of *ds*, *ns* and *gs* in the first line, and the care for the placing of consonants and vowels throughout.

100 *You're* Numbers have a structural significance here: nine lines per stanza, organised according to the number of syllables per line – 8/7/8/7/8/7/8/7/8 in the first stanza, 8/7/8/7/8/7/8/6/8 in the second. But why that divergent 6 in the very line which tells us, 'Right, like a well-done sum'?

101 *The Birth* An alphabetical, rather than numerical, patterning is employed at the heart of this poem, which, however, (coincidentally?) has the same number of lines as Plath's.

102 *Full Moon and Little Frieda* 'Tense' and 'brimming' with observations of both eye and ear, and the seemingly informal versification itself a feat of 'balancing' syllables.

103 and 105 *Death of a Naturalist* and *'A narrow Fellow in the Grass'* Compare the different musics that Heaney and Dickinson create from their separate encounters: the plosive consonants of Heaney's frog chorus; the *o*-sounds in Dickinson's troubling last line.

106 *Recollections after an Evening Walk* Unorthodox as his spelling and punctuation certainly are, Clare employs very few dialect words in this particular poem, and the reader who gets into the swing of it should have no need of a dictionary.

108 *Dover Beach* Ebb and flow.

110 *Lullaby* As has been noted by anthropologists and musicologists, the lullaby is seldom an emotionally uncomplicated thing. Note the interplay here, never merely systematic, between those lines that start on stressed syllables, and those that start on unstressed.

112, 114 and 116 *To His Coy Mistress*, *Dinner with My Mother* and *The Thought-Fox* Deployment, in each, of the repeated word 'now'.

117 *'As kingfishers catch fire'* Not just the standard Italian sonnet rhyme-scheme, but a multitude of internal rhymes and chimes demanding to be heard.

118 *Anahorish* Unrhymed, and yet shot through with the most delicately modulated vowel-music.

119 *Nomad Exquisite* The letter *f*, with appreciable help from *g*, *h* and *m*, carries most of the music here. The sun – our global nomad – is soliloquising.

120, 121 and 122 *To His Son*, *'Thrice toss these oaken ashes in the air'* and *My Cats* Three poems in which the magic number three plays a formal, as well as thematic, part. In Sir Walter Ralegh's charm for the safety of his son, we have the characteristic three quatrains, plus couplet, of the English sonnet (see page 96). Campion's use of three stanzas is surely not accidental, in a poem concerned with magic ritual. And

Stevie Smith's three cats, also from the world of magic, are given three rhyming lines each.

123 *Our Bias* A hybrid of English and Italian sonnet forms (see pages 96 and 7, respectively), with the added surprise of a last line that . . .

124 *'Like as the waves make towards the pebbled shore'* English sonnet, as all Shakespeare's are. The never-predictable placing of assonance and alliteration counterpoints the ostensible single-mindedness of the argument.

125 *Remember* Italian, unsurprisingly, with not just the key word woven through it, but numerous lighter repetitions as well.

126 *The Sunlight on the Garden* As if rhyming at the end of each short line was not difficult enough, MacNeice plants extra rhymes at the beginning of lines 2 and 4 in each stanza.

127 *In the Rhine Valley* A model rondeau – and proof that an antique form can still be used with unhampered freshness.

128 *'Jenny kiss'd me when we met'* Energy imparted by the stress at the beginning of each line.

129 *'So, we'll go no more a-roving'* A more cautious, or less inspired, poet might have avoided using 'so' twice in the first couple of lines. But Byron's repetitions, here and later, are of the essence.

130 *'Fall, leaves, fall'* As many punctuation-marks as words, in the first line.

130 *Sestina* The invention of a French troubadour, the sestina, with its strictly patterned repetition of end-words from stanza to stanza, was initially little more than a showcase for the poet's technical virtuosity. It was not until the twentieth century that poets like Auden and Bishop began to see its expressive potential. Expressing what, though? In this case, something like claustrophobic desperation – though the difficulty of pinning a precise epithet to it is surely part of the point.

133 *'After great pain, a formal feeling comes'* The very few poems Dickinson published in her lifetime had their punctuation

'corrected' editorially. Note how this one begins with rhyming pentameter couplets, loses them in the middle, and then returns to the scheme – albeit qualified with dashes – at the end.

134 *Exposure* Owen was the first English poet to exploit systematically the expressive possibilities – expressive here of numbness, deadlock, futility – of the consonantal rhyme. Lines of six iambic feet, themselves an ungainly rarity in English verse, and the repetition of words and phrases, enhance the effect.

136 *Rain* 'Rain' three times in the first line, then scattered, as either noun or verb, through the remainder of the poem, with unemphatic mid-line rhymes in 'again' and 'pain'.

137 *Frost at Midnight* One of Coleridge's so-called 'conversation poems', though 'thinking-aloud poem' might be more appropriate in this instance. Fluent iambic pentameters accommodate the minutest impressions of sound and sight in what is a masterpiece of tonal organisation. The 'stranger' in line 27 is a name for the sooty film described above.

140 *'Now winter nights enlarge'* Lovely touch of the longer, more relaxed, penultimate line in each stanza. Campion, from whose *Third Book of Airs* this comes, was both poet and musician.

141 *'In my craft or sullen art'* Syllabics again (see page 100), with seven syllables to each line, except for the last line in each stanza, which has six syllables, and, anomalously, the third line of stanza 2 – something to do with 'spindrift'? The trick is to keep the lines moving and lilting without the aid of metre, as Thomas manages to do here.

142 *I Leave This at Your Ear* The reassurance implied by circling back to one's starting-point.

Acknowledgements

The editor and publishers gratefully acknowledge permission to reprint copyright material in this book as follows:

W. H. AUDEN: Faber and Faber Ltd for 'Lullaby' and 'Our Bias' from *Collected Poems* (1976). ELIZABETH BISHOP: 'The Bight' and 'Sestina' from *The Complete Poems 1927–1979* by Elizabeth Bishop, copyright © 1979, 1983 by Alice Helen Methfessel, reprinted by permission of Farrar, Straus & Giroux, Inc. CHARLES CAUSLEY: 'Nursery Rhyme of Innocence and Experience' from *Collected Poems 1951–1975* (Macmillan, 1975) by permission of David Higham Associates Ltd. JOHN CLARE: 'Recollections after an Evening Walk' and 'Clock a Clay' from *John Clare* (The Oxford Authors) edited by Eric Robinson and David Powell (Oxford University Press, 1984), copyright Eric Robinson 1984, reproduced by permission of Curtis Brown Ltd, London. WENDY COPE: Faber and Faber Ltd for 'In the Rhine Valley' from *Serious Concerns* (1992). WALTER DE LA MARE: 'The Listeners' from *Complete Poems of Walter de la Mare* (Faber and Faber, 1969), reprinted by permission of the Literary Trustees of Walter de la Mare, and the Society of Authors as their representative. EMILY DICKINSON: Harvard University Press and the Trustees of Amherst College for 'After great pain, a formal feeling comes', 'I heard a Fly buzz – when I died' and 'A Narrow Fellow in the Grass' from *The Poems of Emily Dickinson*, edited by Thomas H. Johnson (Cambridge, Mass.: The Belknap Press of Harvard University Press), copyright © 1951, 1955, 1979, 1983 by the President and Fellows of Harvard College. CAROL ANN DUFFY: 'Stuffed' from *Mean Time* (Anvil Press Poetry, 1993). T. S. ELIOT: Faber and Faber Ltd for 'Preludes: I', from *Collected Poems 1909–1962* (1963). W. S. GRAHAM: Margaret Snow, literary administrator for Nessie Graham, for 'I Leave This at Your Ear' from *Collected Poems* (Faber, 1979), copyright © The Estate of W. S. Graham. THOMAS HARDY: 'The Phantom Horsewoman' and 'Weathers' from *Collected Poems of Thomas Hardy* (Macmillan, 1930) by kind permission of the Trustees of the Will Trust of Miss E. A. Dugdale, © the Trustees of the Will Trust of Miss E. A. Dugdale, c/o Curtis Brown Ltd. TONY HARRISON: 'The Earthern Lot' from *Selected Poems* (Penguin, 1984). SEAMUS HEANEY: Faber and Faber Ltd for 'Death of a Naturalist' and 'Anahorish' from *New Selected Poems 1966–1987* (1990). A. E. HOUSMAN: The Society of Authors as the Literary Representative of the Estate of A. E. Housman for 'Her Strong Enchantments Failing' from *Collected Poems and Selected Prose*, edited by Christopher Ricks (Allen Lane/Penguin).

TED HUGHES: Faber and Faber Ltd for 'The Thought-Fox', 'Thistles' and 'Full Moon and Little Frieda' from *New Selected Poems 1957–1994* (1995). PHILIP LARKIN: Faber and Faber Ltd for 'The Trees' from *Collected Poems*, edited by Anthony Thwaite (1988). D. H. LAWRENCE: Laurence Pollinger Limited and the Estate of Frieda Lawrence Ravagli for 'The Mosquito' and 'Bavarian Gentians' from *Complete Poems* (Penguin, 1977). HUGH MACDIARMID: Carcanet Press Ltd for 'Empty Vessel' from *Complete Poems of Hugh MacDiarmid*. LOUIS MACNEICE: Faber and Faber Ltd for 'Sunlight on the Garden' and 'Bagpipe Music' from *Collected Poems of Louis MacNeice*, edited by E. R. Dodds (1966). JOHN MASEFIELD: for 'Cargoes' from *Selected Poems* (Heinemann, 1978), permission granted by the Society of Authors as the Literary Representative of the Estate of John Masefield. HAROLD MASSINGHAM: 'Spider' from *Black Bull Guarding Apples* (Longmans, 1965), by kind permission of the author. EDWIN MUIR: Faber and Faber Ltd for 'Merlin' from *Collected Poems* (1960). PAUL MULDOON: Faber and Faber Ltd for 'Quoof' and 'The Birth' from *New Selected Poems 1968–1994* (1996). SYLVIA PLATH: Faber and Faber Ltd for 'Mushrooms' and 'You're' from *Collected Poems*, edited by Ted Hughes (1981). THEODORE ROETHKE: Faber and Faber Ltd for 'My Papa's Waltz' from *Collected Poems of Theodore Roethke*. STEVIE SMITH: James MacGibbon, executor, for 'My Cats' from *Collected Poems*, edited by James MacGibbon (Allen Lane/Penguin, 1975). BERNARD SPENCER: 'Morning in Madrid', © Mrs Anne Humphreys, 1981, reprinted from *Collected Poems*, edited by Roger Bowen (1981), by permission of Oxford University Press. WALLACE STEVENS: Faber and Faber Ltd for 'The Emperor of Ice-Cream' and 'Nomad Exquisite' from *Collected Poems* (1955). DYLAN THOMAS: 'In my craft or sullen art' and 'Do not go gentle into that good night' from *The Poems*, edited by Daniel Jones (Dent, 1971), copyright the Trustees for the Copyrights of Dylan Thomas, c/o David Higham Associates Ltd. ANNA WICKHAM: 'The Fired Pot' from *The Writings of Anna Wickham*, edited by R. D. Smith (Virago, 1984), by kind permission of George W. Hepburn. HUGO WILLIAMS: Faber and Faber Ltd for 'Dinner with My Mother' from *Dock Leaves* (1994). WILLIAM CARLOS WILLIAMS: 'Poem' from *Collected Poems of William Carlos Williams* (1987) by permission of Carcanet Press Ltd. W. B. YEATS: 'Byzantium' from *The Collected Poems of W. B. Yeats* (Macmillan, 1961), by permission of A. P. Watt Ltd on behalf of Michael Yeats. ANDREW YOUNG: 'Passing the Graveyard' from *Poetical Works of Andrew Young*, edited by Edward Lowbury (Secker and Warburg, 1985), by permission of Carcanet Press Ltd.

Index of Poets

Anonymous 16, 79
Matthew Arnold (1822–88) 108
W. H. Auden (1907–73) 110, 123
Hilaire Belloc (1870–1953) 44
Elizabeth Bishop (1911–79) 11, 131
William Blake (1757–1827) 35, 64
Robert Bridges (1844–1930) 55
Emily Brontë (1818–48) 130
Robert Browning (1812–89) 41, 67
Robert Burns (1759–96) 29
George Gordon, Lord Byron (1788–1824) 129
Thomas Campion (1567–1620) 121, 140
Charles Causley (1917–) 75
John Clare (1793–1864) 26, 106
Samuel Taylor Coleridge (1772–1834) 3, 137
Wendy Cope (1945–) 127
William Cornish (early sixteenth century) 18
William Cowper (1731–1800) 95
Walter de la Mare (1873–1956) 84
Emily Dickinson (1830–86) 97, 105, 133
John Donne (1572–1631) 73, 87, 98
Carol Ann Duffy (1955–) 69
T. S. Eliot (1888–1965) 54
W. S. Graham (1918–86) 142
Thomas Hardy (1840–1928) 60, 82
Tony Harrison (1937–) 24
Seamus Heaney (1939–) 103, 118
George Herbert (1593–1633) 23, 50, 88
Thomas Hood (1799–1845) 51
Gerard Manley Hopkins (1844–89) 57, 117
A. E. Housman (1859–1936) 74
Ted Hughes (1930–) 20, 102, 116
Leigh Hunt (1784–1859) 128
Ben Jonson (1572/3–1637) 66, 90
John Keats (1795–1821) 80
Philip Larkin (1922–85) 19
D. H. Lawrence (1885–1930) 8, 31

Richard Lovelace (1618–57/8) 68
Hugh MacDiarmid (1892–1978) 91
Louis MacNeice (1907–63) 47, 126
Andrew Marvell (1621–78) 9, 112
John Masefield (1878–1967) 13
Harold Massingham (1932–) 34
Edwin Muir (1887–1959) 86
Paul Muldoon (1952–) 25, 101
Wilfred Owen (1893–1918) 96, 134
Sylvia Plath (1932–63) 27, 100
Sir Walter Ralegh (1554?–1618) 120
Theodore Roethke (1908–63) 46
Christina Rossetti (1830–94) 125
Sir Walter Scott (1771–1832) 78
William Shakespeare (1564–1616) 15, 70, 124
Christopher Smart (1722–71) 36
Stevie Smith (1902–71) 122
Bernard Spencer (1909–63) 53
Wallace Stevens (1878–1955) 92, 119
Robert Louis Stevenson (1850–94) 14
Alfred, Lord Tennyson (1809–92) 49, 61
Dylan Thomas (1914–53) 99, 141
Edward Thomas (1878–1917) 17, 21, 136
Walt Whitman (1819–92) 58
Anna Wickham (1884–1947) 65
Hugo Williams (1942–) 114
William Carlos Williams (1883–1963) 40
William Wordsworth (1770–1850) 7, 94
W. B. Yeats (1865–1939) 5
Andrew Young (1885–1971) 93

Index of First Lines

A cool small evening shrunk to a dog bark and the clank of a bucket 102
A narrow Fellow in the Grass 105
After great pain, a formal feeling comes 133
Against the rubber tongues of cows and the hoeing hands of men 20
All year the flax-dam festered in the heart 103
As I was walking all alane 79
As kingfishers catch fire, dragonflies draw flame 117
As the cat 40
As the immense dew of Florida 119
At low tide like this how sheer the water is 11
Batter my heart, three-personed God, for you 87
Call the roller of big cigars 92
Clownlike, happiest on your hands 100
Death, be not proud, though some have called thee 98
Die Farben der Bäume sind schön 127
Do not go gentle into that good night 99
Do you remember an Inn 44
Even is come; and from the dark Park, hark 51
Fall, leaves, fall; die, flowers, away 130
Farewell, thou child of my right hand, and joy 90
Faster than fairies, faster than witches 14
Flow on, river! flow with the flood-tide, and ebb with the ebb-tide 58
For I will consider my Cat Jeoffry 36
Had we but world enough, and time 112
Her strong enchantments failing 74
How often have I carried our family word 25
I cannot tell who loves the Skeleton 68
I had a silver penny 75
I heard a Fly buzz – when I died 97
I imagine this midnight moment's forest 116
I leave this at your ear for when you wake 142
I like to toss him up and down 122
I met ayont the cairney 91
I put two yellow peepers in an owl 69
I see you did not try to save 93
I struck the board, and cried, 'No more!' 88
I went to the Garden of Love 64

In my craft or sullen art 141
In our town, people live in rows 65
In the cowslips peeps I lye 26
In Xanadu did Kubla Khan 3
'Is there anybody there?' said the Traveller 34
It's no go the merrygoround, it's no go the rickshaw 47
Jenny kiss'd me when we met 128
Just as the even bell rung we set out 106
Lay your sleeping head, my love 110
Let foreign nations of their language boast 23
Let the bird of loudest lay 70
Like as the waves make towards the pebbled shore 124
My mother is saying 'Now' 114
My 'place of clear water' 118
Not every man has gentians in his house 8
Now winter nights enlarge 140
O Merlin in your crystal cave 86
O, what can ail thee, knight-at-arms 80
O who will show me those delights on high 50
Oh Galuppi, Baldassaro, this is very sad to find 41
Our brains ache in the merciless iced winds that knive us 134
Out of us all 21
Overnight, very 27
Pleasure it is 18
Proud Maisie is in the wood 78
Queer are the ways of a man I know 82
Quinquireme of Nineveh, from distant Ophir 13
Rain, midnight rain, nothing but the wild rain 136
Remember me when I am gone away 125
Room after room 67
Sand, caravans, and teetering sea-edge graves 24
September rain falls on the house 131
Seven o'clock. The seventh day of the seventh month of the year 101
Skirmish of wheels and bells and someone calling 53
So, we'll go no more a-roving 129
Still to be neat, still to be dressed 66
Summer ends now; now, barbarous in beauty, the stooks rise 57
Sweet Suffolk owl, so trimly dight 16
The frost performs its secret ministry 137
The hour-glass whispers to the lion's roar 123
The poplars are felled; farewell to the shade 95
The sea is calm tonight 108
The splendour falls on castle walls 49
The sunlight on the garden 126

The trees are coming into leaf 19
The unpurged images of day recede 5
The whiskey on your breath 46
The winter evening settles down 54
The world is too much with us; late and soon 7
This is the weather the cuckoo likes 60
Three things there be that prosper up apace 120
Thrice toss these oaken ashes in the air 121
Trickling rope-trickster 34
Tyger! Tyger! burning bright 35
'Up, Timothy, up with your staff and away 94
Wee, sleekit, cowrin, tim'rous beastie 29
What passing bells for those who die as cattle 96
When, by thy scorn, O murd'ress, I am dead 73
When did you start your tricks 31
When icicles hang by the wall 15
When men were all asleep the snow came flying 55
Where the remote Bermudas ride 9
With blackest moss the flower-pots 61
Yes. I remember Adlestrop 17

D0249315